The Journey

A Spiritual Autobiography Spanning Two Thousand Years

by

Mary Davies

email mary.davies@btconnect.com
https://www.arransites.co.uk/marydavies

First Published in 1999 by Mary Davies, Ardgowan House, Shore Road, Brodick, Isle of Arran. KA27 8AJ

© 1999 Mary Davies

All rights reserved. No part of this publication may be reproduced, stored in a retrieval system, or transmitted, in any way or form, or by any means, electronic, mechanical, photocopying, recorded or otherwise, without the prior permission of the publisher and copyright holder.

Mary Davies has asserted the moral right to be identified as the author of this work.

British Library Cataloguing in Publication Data.
A catalogue record for this book is available from the British Library.

ISBN: 0 9536398 0 0

Typesetting & Design : Arran Graphics & Computers Ltd, Brodick, Isle of Arran

Printed in the UK by : RCS plc, Retford, Nottinghamshire.

Dedication

To David
the seer

Contents

Introduction

Part One - Past Lives

Chapter 1   Early First Century A.D.
Chapter 2   Third Crusade
Chapter 3   c.1300
Chapter 4   Mid 17th Century
Chapter 5   Mid 18th Century
Chapter 6   Mid 19th Century

Part Two - Present Life

Early Years
Secondary Schooldays
Early Student Days
Student Days in Liverpool
Teaching
Mature Student
Cologne
London Again
Civil Service and Marriage
International Work
The Isle of Arran

Epilogue

Introduction.

When I told my friends that I was writing a book they invariably asked "What is it about?". That is a difficult question to answer. It can be read simply as a group of stories or parables, but my intention in writing it is to illustrate the spiritual evolution of the human soul by revealing my own soul's evolution through six of my previous lives (recovered through regression) and my present life. The past lives may be viewed as fantasies or fact - there is no proof either way - but I admit to having 'embroidered' some details in Part One in order to add interest to the narrative. And truth may be present in fantasy. The story of my present life in Part Two is factual. I have portrayed the evolution as a journey, though there is no tidy, steady progress. We keep making the same mistakes until we learn the lessons that those mistakes offered to teach us.

The style of the writing is deliberately conversational; I address the reader directly in everyday language, and if any reader feels a desire to respond I would welcome their experiences. This book is obviously not the final word on the subject. The journey of the soul is ongoing, there are many paths and many lessons to be learned. The message is one of hope, and freedom from the fear of death.

Mary Davies
Brodick
Isle of Arran.

PART ONE

Chapter 1

The sun was hot. I was glad of the coolness of the big white rock at my back. When night came I would be glad of the shelter of my little cave, but for now it was good to sit and watch the changing light over the lake. The distant hills behind Bethsaida were in shades of soft pearly golds and ochre, the gently rounded tops melting into the intense blue sky. All was reflected in the water of the lake, the blue less blue and the golds more muted. Today the lake was moved only by ripples. Yesterday it was stirred more violently by the dreaded wind from the south, from the desert, bringing heat and sand that cut your face and choked you. That's what I like about Galilee - its changeableness.

It's just as well I'm never bored by it, as it's my whole world. I suppose I'm lucky, really. I could have been stoned. I had sinned, men have right on their side , haven't they. But I ran away and found shelter here, alone, where I can't do any harm and they can forget about me. I manage pretty well. There are wild figs and olives, Simon sometimes gives me a fish and I get milk from the shepherd. The sheep and goats graze in this direction in the mornings and return back along the shore and up the hill in the afternoon. The shepherd, Ezra, is a good soul, but he doesn't like to chat. He doesn't smile and prefers his own company. I don't mind that as he usually smells of sheep, but he's handsome enough, with his flashing eyes and curly beard. He could set my heart fluttering if it weren't dead, numb with the pain of the past. But it's best not to think about it. The fishermen are different. They love gossip. Though they're always busy fishing and don't spend much time in the village, they get all their gossip when they go home to their families at night. But for now it's too hot in the midday sun, nothing stirs but the gentle lulling water at my feet, and I can rest and dream.

Dream of what I once was, when I lived in Tiberius. It was a good life in its way. Mother always kept our little house clean, shining white in the sunlight, and she wasn't a bad cook. Aaron and Joshua were lively and difficult to handle, but they were young. I wonder if they are still so rebellious, now that they must be grown up. I suppose we were all rebels in our different ways. Father was a dreamer, a potter, but he never stirred himself to make enough pots to keep the family and pay the taxes. So can you blame us, mother and me, for earning what we could in the only way possible? Mother never went with other men, but she encouraged me, and Father never knew. I was pretty then, young, proud of my glossy black hair. Men liked my curves, and they were willing to pay to enjoy them. Perhaps they also enjoyed my company, as I was a lively talker in those days. But it all came to an end when Jacob, the fat greasy one who rarely washed and was avoided by everybody, bragged about his 'conquest'. He hadn't the wit to realise that I was using him as he was using me. But unfortunately his bragging started all the unpleasantness. Father heard about it and was furious. He said he would never be able to hold his head up in the town again, but I expect he also felt guilty that his idleness had driven me to it. Poor Mother pleaded for understanding and compassion but no - I was guilty and must take my punishment. So of course I ran, at night, secretly, even mother knowing nothing. Somehow I survived and here I am, just far enough away from the town to be tolerated so long as I stay out of sight. I keep myself clean, though my skirts have got torn in the thorn bushes and my hair is no longer glossy.

Simon and Andrew are rowing across from Bethsaida. They've been fishing on the way and will sell their catch for a better price on this side in the Capernaum market. Andrew's a nice lad, but Simon bosses him. He's quite a character, is Simon. The others call him Rocky, as he's heavy and thick-set, but it's also a joke because he's more like shifting sand than a rock. He's impulsive and unreliable, but kind, and I appreciate his kindness; not many people have been kind to me in my life. Zebedee is already on the shore. His sons are out with the boat, but he will be fishing close to the beach. They don't notice me as I creep along the beach. My white robes blend into the whiteness of the pebbles and rocks on the shore, and if I get close enough I will hear their voices magnified over the water. Zebedee is grumbling as usual. "Who does he think he is, this man from Nazareth? What right has he to disrupt all our lives? Why can't he stay and upset people in Nazareth? What am I to do without my two boys? I'm too old to man the boat alone, and without the fishing how am I to live? And James and John - they must have taken leave of their senses to want to go off with this preacher. How are they going to live? I can perhaps understand John, he was always the dreamy one, but I thought James had more sense. And what is their mother going to say? We shall both need a full explanation when the boys come home tonight. I can't let them go with my blessing until I know something more about this preacher. Is he just passing through Galilee and will let my boys come home when he's gone, or are they going to be lost to me forever? Woe is me - what am I to do?" As Zebedee went on chuntering to himself, Simon and Andrew were nearing the beach and I could hear them talking about the preacher too. He seems to be causing quite a stir.

They don't see me, but I can see Andrew preparing to land the boat, and Simon is gathering together the nets full of fish. It seems to have been a profitable crossing. Simon is talking, "It's best if you go first to the dinner-party tonight. Sarah's mother invited both of us to meet this Jesus, but then she fell sick. I don't much care for the old woman but the party's still going ahead and I'd like to see what sort of fellow this Jesus is. I'll go across the lake again, pick up Sarah so she can help at the dinner, I'll do one more fishing trip as the fish are so plentiful, take them to the market and then join you all later at mother-in-law's house."

Andrew's saying, "But you said you were very keen to meet Jesus. People say he does miracles, makes sick people well just by looking at them or something. And I'd rather we went together. I'm not sure I believe in miracles and magic." "No, you go ahead and I'll follow later. You'll probably enjoy it. Mother-in-law does provide plenty of good food as a rule, if she's up to it. Behave yourself and tell her I'll be along presently." This is Simon, being bossy as usual, though I'm sure Andrew can look after himself.

I wonder if I could have a look at this Jesus? I know whereabouts the house is and I might be able to get a glimpse of him. I don't believe in miracles but I'd like to see one being done. Goodness knows, there's need of miracles to cure all the sick people around here; the rabbis and the wise men don't seem to be able to do anything. There was another man, called John, but I don't think he was up to much - he just poured water over people and they were supposed to feel better. But somehow this Jesus is different. I feel drawn to him in some way. Ridiculous, really, as I've no time for religion. It was religious people who wanted to stone me, because of their guilt and fear. I'll follow Andrew and see what happens. If I go carefully and dodge behind the rocky outcrops on the hill no one will notice me. In Capernaum I'm just nobody anyway, and the house is on this side of the city so I won't have to walk down the streets. I wouldn't dare do that, in my disgrace and torn skirts. It will be enough if I just catch a glimpse of the preacher and then I'll go away again. Why do I feel like this? It's most odd. I don't understand myself but I feel as if I have to meet this man, though I'm sure he doesn't want to meet me.

It's easy to run from rock to rock, keeping Andrew in sight, and it's pleasant up on the hill with the cool breeze of evening on my face. It doesn't take long before I see the first houses of the city, glowing rosy-coloured in the evening light. I think Sarah's mother's name is Miriam, like mine, and her house is one of these. Andrew is heading for the second one on the right, and I can already smell tasty herbs and spices, food like mother used to make but which I haven't tasted in years. Ah, well, the smell's good and I'll have to make do with that. Andrew's gone inside now and I can get nearer to the doorway. It's open, no door, so I can see inside. There are men (Andrew among them) standing with their backs to me., so it's difficult to see what is going on. But I can imagine the guests reclining around the table piled high with luscious food and fresh fruits, really mouth-watering. But where is Jesus? It won't be possible to see him in all this crowd. What a waste of effort and what a fool I am to think I could see the preacher.

But suddenly, somebody moves away and I see his feet. He must be reclining on his left elbow with his back to me. Only feet, sore but clean-washed. Why does this affect me so? What is happening to me? I've never felt like this before. Something's happening to my inside. I can hardly breathe. God of Abraham, who is this man? It feels as if Jehovah has lifted me up, squeezed me dry, shaken me, dipped me in pure living water, then wrapped me around with divine love. It's as if the man knows all about me; I don't even have to ask for forgiveness, his love makes forgiveness superfluous. And oh! this love! It fills me and fills the universe. It will drive me mad. I can't contain it or sustain it. Nobody has ever loved me before, and now I am destroyed by a love too great. My human-ness is not strong enough to bear it, my spirit is too weak. Where can I go? What can I do to rid myself of this love. It's more than I can bear..... The lake, my lake! It will receive me and maybe cleanse my spirit, that I may some day be able to accept this love. The lake is friendly, as I sink beneath its surface to a blessed peace.

A blessed peace, but where did this light come from? It's spreading and spreading, as if it fills the universe, a brilliant white light more powerful than the sun and yet it doesn't hurt my eyes. My eyes? I don't seem to have any eyes. And I don't have a body either. What has happened to me? This can't be heaven. It should be hell.
I have sinned, terribly. My life was wasted, with nothing accomplished, and then I threw it away. I don't deserve this peace and the love which I feel pulsating through the light. And am I seeing things or is there a Being of Light within the light? Is it an angel come to condemn me? "I do not condemn you, or judge you. You are here to experience something divine, non-judgemental love, perchance to take back to Earth some memory of it. Learn diligently while you are here. There is much that you will forget and you will make many more mistakes, but my wisdom and love are always available at your call. And, however much you forget, your soul will always yearn for unity with me, the unity which can only be achieved by love. So go, when you are ready, back to my beloved Earth, and continue to learn to live by love."

Chapter 2

The sun was hot. The washing had dried quickly, smelling fresh and sweet, so I had enjoyed the sunshine and the heat by the washing stones at the river's edge. The river was full, as the westerly wind had brought us a lot of rain and some of the houses in the lower part of the town had been flooded. All the women at the washing stones were hoping we might have a fine summer and a good harvest. My friend Margaret was there, always laughing, as if she found life a great joke. I don't find life a joke. It's very serious, and I told her of my big decision.

"I ask you, Margaret, what sort of life would it be for me married to a tanner? Tom is a good man and I know he loves me. The other girls admire him for his good looks; I know he's tall and slender, fair and clean shaven, better looking than most of the other young men of the town. Although he looks too frail for the hard work of pounding and stretching the leather, nobody can make such fine soft leather as Tom, and he gets a good price for the finest pieces which the scribes use in the monastery. So I agree, tanning is a good living and Tom is a good man, but I can't see myself as a tanner's wife. I'm sure I could never get used to the stinking smell of the tannery, the muddy lanes and the dirt in our town, and the little wooden house shared with his widowed mother which is all I could expect Tom to provide. No, I want something better. My father doesn't need me. I'm young and healthy, I know I'm pretty with curly fair hair and blue eyes, I have strong arms and I'm a good worker, so I think they'll be glad to accept me as a servant at the Castle. I'm sorry to leave you, Margaret, but if I like it there, perhaps you'll follow me".

Margaret replied "I don't think I shall be tempted to work for the invaders and I think you're making a big mistake. Tom loves you and, as you admit, he's a good man. You could do a lot worse." "But I could do a lot better and I don't care if you think I'm being disloyal. These Normans have a better way of living and I want to share it. The Castle looks splendid there on top of the hill, new and white in the sunlight. I wonder what it's like inside, better than our miserable little huts I'm sure.

And it certainly won't be washed away by the floods".

Margaret was not convinced. "Remember, Alice," she said "They are the enemy. They invaded and conquered us and many of our men suffered. John Thatcher got a spear in his side if you remember. They demolished the houses on the hillside and forced the people to move away." But I protested. "It was so easy to conquer us, we had no defence really. The palisade was of wood and very flimsy. I know, because father was constantly called on to repair it. Perhaps because it was so easy to conquer us there was no need for any really fierce fighting and so they haven't treated us too badly. At least they have strengthened the palisade and with the hillside cleared it will be easy for them to repel or discourage the barbarians from the north. So the town will be protected too. And, as they are so clever at building in stone perhaps they will rebuild our bridge in stone so it doesn't wash away so often."

So it was that I came to the Castle. It was dark inside but there was a wonderful view through the narrow slits in the walls. I was high up and could see our little town down below, looking very small with its scattered little houses. I could see the whole valley, the hills where the building stone comes from, and the river winding its way to the sea. This first impression of the Castle was exciting, like being a bird high above the ground. To get up so high there were stairs in the thickness of the walls. I'd never seen such thick strong walls. The tower was like one house on top of another; several of our little houses would have fitted into each of the great halls on each floor, and then there were other rooms, much smaller, actually inside the walls. It was really wonderful. I wished Margaret could have seen it.

My overseer was called Marguerite (I knew this was French for Margaret as I'd already learned something of their language). She was older than me with dark hair and eyes, rather small I thought, but strong-looking and quite kindly. I liked her as soon as I saw her and we were soon to become friends. "I shall call you Alicia," she said, "It's the French name for Alice." Alicia! I savoured it on my tongue and liked it, so elegant and refined! She continued "Your work here is to keep the floors clean, fetch water from the well and keep the fire going with logs. It's not easy, carrying logs up the narrow twisting stairs but you look strong." I gladly agreed to do all this and further told her that I could sew, and she said that perhaps I may be asked to make some dresses later.

The lord of the Castle was away when I started work there. They said he was a duke and his name was Richard, like the King. But his lady was present. Her name was Blanche and she was a very fine lady, slim and dark with high cheekbones and delicate hands that had obviously never had to do any hard work. But she appeared to be very unhappy. She rarely smiled and snapped at the servants if we crossed her path, spending most of the day with her embroidery in the little room in the south wall. So I tried not to have anything to do with her, and took my orders only from Marguerite. I was becoming quite fluent in her language and she understood that I was keen to learn Norman ways. The other servants, men and women, were all dark-haired and came from Normandy or France with the duke and his soldiers. They had fascinating stories to tell of their far-off countries and their different customs. How I wished I could travel to see these wonders!

But the duke returned eventually and I saw him for the first time as he came through the Great Hall as I was a replenishing the fire. He was a tall man, broad-shouldered, strong and vigorous. I like strong men. Tom always looked so weak. After a few days I was aware that he'd noticed me - not too difficult, really, as I was the only fair-haired woman in the Castle. He said, "How is it that I find a fair-haired woman in the Castle, and with such beautiful blue eyes?" I told him I had come from the little town down by the river and had chosen to work at the Castle. I could see he was much impressed and his eyes followed me about whenever I had occasion to go to the Great Hall where he normally spent his time, giving orders and checking accounts and land holdings. Of course, the fire needed replenishing very frequently!

One day he said "I don't like to see you in that drab dress, it doesn't do justice to your eyes. You need to wear blue." I protested that I was merely a servant and didn't have a blue dress. "I can remedy that", he said, "I have a length of silk which is the exact shade of blue as your eyes. It came from the other side of the world, brought to me by merchants from Venice, and it's so precious I keep it in my treasury room above, but if you will meet me in the little room in the west wall at sunset tomorrow I will give it to you so you can make yourself a dress and wear it to please me". I was so excited and proud. Pure silk, so precious and especially for me, as a favour from the duke. Of course I lay with him after that, partly in gratitude but partly because I really admired his strength and felt sorry that (as he said) his wife was a cold woman and would never give him the son he longed for. Every man wants a son, it's only natural, so I was happy to serve him and eventually I bore him a male child. We called him William. Such a happy child, as he played about the Castle; he had my blue eyes and his father's boldness and courage. It rejoiced my heart to see him growing so handsome and strong. But as he grew, so the duke demanded more from him, training him in military duties and leadership "to be a worthy son of a duke," as he said.

That was how I gradually got pushed aside. I'd done my duty in providing him with a son. His wife, Blanche, in her unhappiness and bitterness had finally retired to a nunnery which her father had founded in the next valley, and now he could have any woman he wished. My blue eyes no longer excited him and I kept out of his way. Men are not to be trusted, I decided, and wished I'd never gone there as a servant. I could have been mistress in my own home in the town, even though it would have been small. The living conditions in the town were improved, the streets well-ordered, the bridge had been rebuilt in stone and the river diverted so it didn't flood. If I'd married Tom life would have got gradually easier and we would have had our children around us. Marguerite was right when she said "You were a silly child when you came to the Castle, blinded by false glamour and the desire for material things instead of the things that matter. And now you are having to pay for it all."

The day arrived when the payment became almost too much to bear. Being some distance from the city we were always glad to welcome wayfarers at the Castle, as they bring us news from distant places. One day a travelling Friar came, a preaching Dominican, and he told us, "I've come from London, working my way along the rivers, and all the talk in the city is about Jerusalem. It seems that the infidel has seized it again and they're destroying all the holy places. There's great activity and excitement in London and in Westminster, as King Richard and the French are organising a crusade to drive the infidel out of Jerusalem and set up the Christian standard there again. We can't tolerate that such holy Christian places are being desecrated by infidels. Soldiers who have come back from fighting there say the enemy are cruel and fierce warriors, sparing no prisoners and killing even women and children. So it's obviously our Christian duty to go and rescue Jerusalem from such a fate."

So Duke Richard ordered all the men who owed him military duties to report to the Castle including, of course, my William. He was eager to go. It was an adventure for him, he would see foreign lands and experience crossing the sea in a ship, he would enjoy the comradeship of other knights and above all he would be able to test his strength and courage against an enemy. How foolish men are and how they break our hearts! But I must admit they made a brave and splendid sight as they assembled and filed out to war. Great strong horses, dogs yelping at their hooves, the men resplendent in their armour, the standards fluttering and the duke in command at the head. And my son William at his side looking so handsome. I was so proud of him in spite of my aching heart. May God grant that they come back as proudly, was my fervent prayer.

And so Marguerite and I were left in the Castle with the junior servants. Some of the more mature and experienced women were obliged to go with the army, an arduous duty, but they had to take provisions and ensure that the men were well fed on the journey and fighting fit when they reached Jerusalem. Most of the active men went with the duke, and the remaining men were old or sick. Because of that the work in the Castle became harder and heavier, and I became daily more and more tired. I felt sorry for myself and even more sorry for Marguerite; she was in charge and responsible for the smooth running of the Castle's affairs, but she was even older than me and had grown fat and stiff in her joints, and had to rely on young girls who didn't care and were slapdash in their work. The fire in the Great Hall was seldom lit now, as nobody was strong enough or cared enough to carry the logs up the stairs. It was a sad time but, when we had free moments, Marguerite and I used to go to the little chapel over the Castle entrance and sit there in peace, away from the worries of work. There was no priest any more but it was a place of tranquility where we could think of happier days and what might have been.

What a strange thing love is. It can mean so many things. I'd known Tom's love in my youth but didn't value it. Later I realised Duke Richard never loved me, it was only lust and self-interest that drove him to seduce me. Tom made no effort to persuade me not to go to the Castle, and Richard just cast me aside when he'd no further use for me. No wonder I came to despise men. So these little interludes of musing in the chapel became increasingly important to me, as the daily life of the Castle became more onerous and unpleasant. I was no longer young and slim, and would not have been able to wear my blue silk dress even if I had had the heart to do so. I had trouble with my breathing, my steps were slow and I scarcely slept. It was such a worry, wondering what was happening to my William. From time to time we gave hospitality to travelling craftsmen who brought us news from the city, of fierce fighting in Jerusalem with the superior forces of the infidel, whose leader they said was called Saladin. When will all this bloodshed end, and our men return?

But at last the bloodshed did come to an end. We heard that our brave soldiers had been defeated and driven back. Many had been killed and the survivors were coming home demoralised and in disarray. We watched eagerly for their arrival, anxious to see if our loved ones were among them. Alas, my William was not with them. His comrades said he had died of his wounds but had fought bravely. Did they think that was any consolation to me? How can God allow these evil things to happen? What have I done to deserve such pain? I bore my son in pain, only for him to be killed by heathens in a strange land far from home. This pain at my heart is suffocating me. I can't breathe. Everything around me is going dark. I'm falling, falling...

It was all dark, but what is this light? And it's oh!, so peaceful. And there is no more pain. I can rest here and feel the peace soaking into me. But where am I? Is this heaven? It's not like the priests said. I don't see any angels playing harps and no heavenly choirs. But it's good to rest in this peace. Somehow there is a sort of lovingness in this peace, as if I'm held in invisible loving arms. And it's as if my William were here, though I can't see him. I can only feel his presence and in a way I don't understand I'm aware that he is smiling. Shouldn't there have been a judgement? I don't deserve to be in heaven. I was wilful, made wrong choices all my life, rejected the genuine in favour of the false, I was greedy for material things, selfish, and neglected to help people when I had the opportunity. I could have used my influence over Richard to make life easier for the other servants and I could have helped them with advice instead of merely criticising them for incompetence. I might even have had a kind thought for Blanche instead of condemning her for her lack of affection for Richard. She had been forced by her father to marry a man she didn't love in order to increase his land holdings and prestige, so I understand now how she must have felt. And I can even understand Richard. It was so important to him as the duke that all his wealth in land and property should be passed on to a son and his son in succession. Strange how I can understand how such things seem to be important on earth and at the same time to be aware of how unreal they are. This here (wherever it is) is the true reality and somehow I must try to take it back to Earth. I shall forget again, I must learn through earthly experience, but perhaps something of this peace and love will remain with me as I return again.

Chapter 3

The sun was hot. I was tending the garden, weeding the vegetables. At least, that's what I was supposed to be doing. In reality I was simply daydreaming, enjoying the shade under the arbour of Etruscan honeysuckle, smelling sweetly as it cascaded over the bench where I was sitting. The fruit was hanging heavy on the trees, the cypress trees were like dark sentinels surrounding our priory on top of our Tuscan hill, with its wide views over the countryside. Life was very pleasant. But my reverie was rudely interrupted by Brother Damien who came running and out of breath to summon me into the presence of Father Sylvanus. The wishes of Father Sylvanus were not to be ignored and I hurried back indoors to his study - an all-too -familiar occurrence for me, I'm afraid, as I was always being called to account for my behaviour. I hadn't been in the Order very long and found it hard to shake off my worldly ways.

The Father was a short, portly man of middle age, with kindly humorous lines to his face, but nevertheless he ruled our fraternity with a rod of iron. To be fair, the punishments he doled out usually fitted the crimes and reflected his sense of humour, and I wondered what he had in store for me, to punish me for my idleness.

"Brother Anselm" he said, on this occasion with a wicked gleam in his eye, the lines of his face stiff with displeasure. "As you're so full of youthful energy and enthusiasm for action you shall be given the responsibility of going out into the wider world to preach the Gospel to the poor, as our Order was founded to do. Specifically. you are to take nothing with you, making your way northwards over the mountains towards the river Rhine, and proceed down the Rhine until you reach Cologne. How you make your way there depends on your own initiative, and you will find hospitality wherever you may, with members of our Order, local clerics or perhaps the peasantry. I am entrusting you with a letter of commendation to His Eminence the Prince-Bishop of Cologne and the Palatinate. When you have delivered the letter and fulfilled your mission you may return to Tuscany, wiser and more mature in spirit."

I was surprised and delighted. I thought it was so wonderful to be going out into the world. What famous places I would see, what interesting people I would meet and what exciting adventures I would have! I couldn't imagine, in my ignorant youth, that the distances were so great, the hazards so dangerous, and that the task Father Sylvanus had given me would take me most of my life to fulfil. But that's how it all started.

I had my last meal in the refectory with the other Brothers and set off. I was sorry to leave my friends the younger Brothers, but felt really very superior. They were to spend their lives serving the poor people of Tuscany, which is hardly the wider world. I was proud to be entrusted with the momentous task the Father had given me (I was very proud in those days and didn't appreciate the seriousness of the mission). But I was off to see the world, at least as far as Cologne, resplendent in my clean grey habit and new sandals for the occasion.

Northwards lay the mountains, enticing and frightening, but first came the road to Florence. I had been there once before, but that was before the Cathedral was founded. Now I would see how the building was progressing. They said our painter Giotto had been appointed as architect. He'd done some fine paintings in Assissi, though they were not to everyone's taste, and I couldn't see why a painter should be thought to be any good as a builder. There wasn't much to see when I got there, only foundations, so I explored the back streets by the Arno. There were some interesting taverns there, serving good wine, and there were many poor people, too poor to buy food but forgetting their misery in drink. I thought to preach to them of the saving grace of Jesus, but a scuffle broke out between Guelph and Ghibelline supporters. I am ashamed that, in my hot-headed and thoughtless youth, I got drawn into the skirmish, on the side of the Guelphs of course, and gave at least one Ghibelline supporter a good thrashing. It was worth the penance!

It was a pity there weren't as yet many settlements of Poor Clares where I could get food and lodging. They were renowned for their good food in Tuscany, but as I journeyed farther north I had to rely on local people or sometimes priests, though quite often I found priests to be hostile to the idea of a wandering preacher. Perhaps they were jealous or even ashamed that they cared so little for the poor.

I didn't much care for Bologna. It was a city of clever

intellectuals, proud of their university and their learning, not inclined to be charitable to a humble friar. But even here I found poverty. Our blessed Francis would have drawn great crowds to hear him preach salvation, but I had little skill in preaching and could only try to console the poor widows and orphaned children, talk to them of Jesus' compassion and listen to their woes. And then move on. But the poor are everywhere generous in their hospitality and I must admit I enjoyed the best they could offer me. I got very hungry being out all day and really looked forward to being entertained by a good cook and being offered a soft bed. These material comforts became increasingly welcome as I approached the mountains. It was unbelievably cold and I hated the snow and the threatening harshness of the landscape. The mountains were truly awesome, I thought, and I missed the softness of our southern landscape, the bright flowers and the friendly birds. Here, everything seemed hard, though the valleys were lush enough and the food here was better. I had been lucky to get through the mountain passes without being waylaid by robbers. It was a hazardous undertaking to cross the mountains, and many travellers suffered both deprivation and robbery. But I was strong and resilient, and of course had nothing to tempt a robber.

    I was very glad when some merchants I met, who had journeyed from Venice and eastern lands beyond, proposed that I joined them in the boat they hired on Lake Constance, which they said would bring me to the Rhine. Unfortunately they didn't say they were going to accuse one another of theft and become so agitated that we nearly capsized. This time at least I didn't join in the quarrel. Otherwise this was a welcome interlude as I was becoming very tired by this time, and somewhat weary of preaching to the poor, to tell you the truth. However much I cared about them, and I did care, there was nothing I could do to alleviate their poverty. I could only assure them of a loving Heavenly Father and interpret for them the pictures and statues they saw in their churches. The old pictures of stiff, stern Virgins and solemn infants were being superseded by more natural human - looking figures, which I preferred. I heard that this New Age was initiated by a Dominican called Eckhart, but whether that was true or not it was certainly in the spirit of Franciscans, and there were some interesting new statues being sculpted for some of the more wealthy churches. I later saw one of the Madonna and Child in Cologne which reminded me of a Poor Clare sister (Sister Agatha, a beautiful woman with a warm smile and kindly eyes - I really liked her and could imagine her as a graceful swaying Madonna). However, I mustn't think of Poor Clares but continue my story. I had many other adventures, dodging local insurrections among the city states and avoiding the tolls and taxes extorted by petty dukes and princes. My sandals had several times been replaced and my habit was a much darker grey and threadbare by the time I reached Cologne.

It was a very impressive city, worthy of a Prince-Bishop, with a busy crossing over the Rhine, a thriving commercial centre and a splendid new Cathedral which would still take many years to complete. I found very comfortable lodgings in a new monastery - everything really modern, warm, with plenty of good food. Cologne struck me as being a very wealthy city, ruled by a powerful Prince who at the same time ruled the Church hierarchy. Between Church and State there was little freedom for the ordinary burgher, but I detected no imminent insurrection, so I couldn't be tempted to take sides and get into trouble. I felt the power, though, as I was definitely treated as something beneath contempt, being a humble Franciscan from Tuscany. Many times I pleaded with the officials for an audience with the Bishop and was told to wait. Apparently, although the wealthy churchmen were keen to employ the most modern artists and sculptors they drew the line at the modern ideas of Francis. They also frowned on the Dominican Eckhart I believe.

At last, however, my turn came for an audience with His Eminence. I was ushered into a large ornate room glowing with gilt, the walls covered with exquisite frescoes. Comfort and opulence were the words that best described it, in my mind. The prelate extended his hand towards me, and as I made obeisance at his feet and kissed his ring I noticed his fat white fingers and thought how many rich dinners he must have had and he certainly would not have survived our near ship-wreck on the lake. His weight would have sunk the boat. At length he spoke, looking first at the letter I had brought and then at me, with a quizzical sort of look as if he was trying not to laugh. I couldn't imagine why such an august person would be amused, and there was no amusement in his tone as he said, quite coldly in fact. "You have fulfilled your mission. You may go now." And that was that! I was stunned. I had expected some kind of recognition for my effort, or a reply to the letter, or an invitation to a meal at the palace refectory. But nothing! I slunk away and when I had recovered my equilibrium I determined that now that I was free of obligation I would not hurry back home but would enjoy my worldly travels as long as I could. In spite of my treatment at the palace I liked Cologne. The people were friendly with a light-hearted sort of gaiety that appealed to me. So I enjoyed the music and the art, watched the builders at work on the Cathedral and counted the many boats going up and down the river.

But eventually I realised time was passing, I was growing older and beginning to feel the pull of old familiar surroundings, so I started to wend my way southwards again. My familiarity with the people of Cologne had given me access to information about shipping on the Rhine, so this time I was wise enough to ask for free passage from sympathetic traders and thus proceed from town to town. Often I was called upon to help with the oars, as it was hard work going against the strong current, but at least it was more comfortable than walking. This time there were no quarrelsome traders but when we reached Bingen and had to pay the toll I was rowed to the shore and left, because I had no money. The boatman said he had done me a favour and the least I could do was to pay the toll. Occasionally I did have a little money, though of course it wasn't allowed under our Rule. But there were occasions when I had listened to someone's problems and given them my advice and a blessing they then rewarded me with enough money to buy some bread. I had learned a little more skill as a preacher by that time, too, and was gratified by this success. I was even beginning to enjoy preaching, and, as each time was to a different audience I was able to keep refining the same theme - the love of God for his creation - my old idleness repeating itself no doubt.

In spite of lingering in the softer living conditions of the valleys the time came when, inevitably, I had to face the mountains again. This time I joined a group of goldsmiths who were returning to Florence after successfully selling their wares in the northern markets. They were a cheerful group and told interesting stories of how they fashioned such beautiful and intricate work that I had seen earlier in Florence. But this time the mountain pass held more danger. Just as we were nearing a particularly narrow gorge - the frowning cliffs at either side filled me with terror - a band of robbers burst out from behind a huge boulder, attacked us all with staves and rocks, felled us to the ground and took everything that the craftsmen had earned. Although I had no worldly wealth to lose I was beaten and bruised like the rest. We made a sorry sight as we gathered ourselves together and continued on our way, limping and sore.

But at length we arrived in Florence. I said farewell to my new friends and continued on my way to rejoin my old fraternity. It was not a triumphal homecoming. I was bedraggled, my habit torn and dirty, my sandals worn out (again), my body bent and old, my face worn and lined. There was little in the way of a welcome. Father Sylvanus had died years ago, many of the Brothers had been dispersed to guide other Friaries and the newer younger Brothers had scarcely heard of me. But they all tolerated me, gave me hospitality and treated me with a certain amount of respect and honour.

So that is how I passed my remaining days, in good weather sitting on the bench under the honeysuckle arbour, thinking of how it all started. I'd travelled many miles and had many experiences and adventures, would Father Sylvanus have considered I had returned "wiser and more mature in spirit"?

"Well, and are you wiser and more mature in spirit?" But this isn't Father Sylvanus. It's an angel of light, smiling, inviting me to speak. What can I say? I don't feel any wiser and I know I'm not spiritually mature. I've done many foolish things but I've also learned a few things. I've learned not to jump into other people's quarrels, I've learned to listen to the problems of the poor, I've learned to preach the Gospel in many different circumstances, and I've learned compassion. That's all, I think. "And what more do you think you need to learn?" I thought the angel should be telling me that, but I said I was ashamed of my gluttony, my desire for a soft life, my wanderlust, and my thoughts of Sister Agatha. Then, I can't express how wonderful it was, this shining angel of light led me to a most beautiful garden where other souls and other angels were strolling about among the flowers apparently talking and discussing. And the angel invited me to ask anything I wished, as the angels were there to teach me whatever I desired to learn, to equip me for my next return to Earth. It was also explained to me that, though I may choose the situation and the family into which I would be born, I would gradually lose the memory of this state of bliss as long as I continued to make bad choices or allowed the world's materialism to dominate me. The angel's last admonition, with a smiling farewell "Hold fast to that which is good."

Chapter 4

The sun was hot. High above, the sky was a cloudless blue but here, under the trees at the water's edge, the sunlight was dappled and dancing in the gentle breeze. The beech tree at my back felt firm and somehow comforting. Goodness knows I would need support and comfort in the future. But now I enjoyed the tranquility of being alone with the golden carpet of last year's leaves and the splashing of the stream on the rocks at my feet. I should have been employed in writing a dissertation on 'The Importance of Ritual in Modern Life' but I was half thinking, half dreaming of my latest poem. I wasn't sure about the last verse and had come to this place of peace, a far corner of my father's estate, to think about the right words to express my feelings. My feelings and my poems were in response to the sights and sounds of nature, tranquil scenes such as this by the woodland stream, or the wild turbulence of a storm on the high moorland, when the purple-grey clouds were angrily riven by flashes of lightning and the earth seemed to open itself up to the sky so that earth and sky were one, and I was one with both.

I'd heard of the Reverend Herrick who had just published a very fine poem, but I knew I was not so gifted as he and could never combine a clerical career with writing poetry. Being a cleric did not appeal to me, but I felt impelled to write. Something inside me needed to be expressed and I could no longer ignore the inner voice which was telling me that an academic career was not the right way for me. I must follow my conviction and continue to write poetry. It was a hard decision in many ways - how would I live, how could I support a wife, what would be my standing in society. But on the other hand, once the decision was made the relief and feeling of freedom compensated for all the former worries.

My wonderful Mary made my decision possible of course. When I told her of my proposal to give up the academic study she said "I knew you were not happy studying all those books, Jonathan, and I can't be happy either unless you are content in your career. We will be together in this decision. Somehow we will manage until your poetic talents are fully acknowledged. I have faith in you and when we are married I will make you a good wife. You will have a peaceful home-life and the support you need, and I shall enjoy your presence at home. If you were to obey your father's wishes and become an ordained parson, you would not be happy, I know, and I think your decision is a wise one. Should we go together to tell your parents?". This was my Mary, knowing intuitively the right thing to do.

My parents were good people, well-respected in the county. They were wealthy landowners and had good family connections; this was part of my problem, as I was naturally expected to act my part in following the family traditions - the eldest son trained to run the estate and the younger son to enter the Church. Father was content enough with my brother Robert, who managed the estate very efficiently, but I anticipated he would be angry with me for abandoning my studies at the seminary. And both parents, I felt, would be angry and disappointed at my intention to marry Mary. She was the daughter of our head gardener and lived on the estate. We had met one day in the garden when I was savouring the heady perfume of the damask roses and she came past me with a basket of fragrant herbs which she had been gathering. "My father has told me a great deal about plants, especially herbal plants that can be used for cooking or as medication, and I very much enjoy working with living things in the open air", she said. She was not beautiful, but wiry and strong with an open expression and laughing eyes. Her intelligence and sensitivity captivated me at that first meeting and our love grew as we discovered how much we shared the deeper things in life. We knew we belonged together and the natural decision to marry was taken some time before approaching our respective parents.

But the time came when we went hand-in-hand to my father in his study. He stood there, every inch the landed gentleman, somewhat portly of figure and florid in complexion. "Well, what is this about your abandoning your studies? And writing poetry of all things. Is this all your expensive education has led to? I had great hopes for you. My contacts with patrons could have procured for you a lucrative living in a pleasant part of the country, with a good parsonage house and an easy way of life. I can't understand you turning your back on all this. As if this wasn't bad enough, you also decide to marry beneath you". This was embarrassing, and as if to acknowledge his indelicacy, father turned to Mary and continued in a gruff tone, as if ashamed but unable to apologise "Your father serves me well and I daresay you are a good soul but hardly the sort my son should marry. His brother Robert is marrying Lady Barbara next month - a good match which will amalgamate our neighbouring estates. But to marry for love hmph! - nonsense!"By this time his anger had abated a little and he went on "But no son of mine shall go begging. You shall have one of the estate cottages rent free, but after that you must make your own way as well as you can. At least you are not meddling in politics, it could be dangerous to be on the wrong side. We don't know where we are these days - a King one day and a so-called Protector the next. What is the country coming to?" With that the interview was over.

It had gone rather better than expected, and we approached mother with lighter hearts. Her silvery head was bent over delicate embroidery as we entered her drawing room; this was the very embroidery which my Mary had helped to fashion because she had brought wild flowers which mother had used in her design. So the two were acquainted, but mother had never, I'm sure, contemplated accepting Mary as a daughter-in-law. However, it was not too difficult to persuade mother that Mary would be of practical and sensible help to me. "You know, mother, a county girl would never be happy with me, nor I with her. And surely you desire my happiness? Mary is sensible and wise, she will keep my feet on the ground and run our household efficiently and economically." And so it was agreed.

We married quietly and settled into a little cottage of stone and slate in the local tradition, on the edge of the wood and not too far from the city of Westchester, which was to figure so disastrously in our future. But it was pleasant enough at the beginning. Father's manor house lay below the woods, on a headland where the river met the sea, but the cottage was convenient for Mary to visit her father (her mother had died of the plague when she was a child) and to help him in the gardens. We grew our own vegetables and had a few hens; Mary earned a little cheese and butter from time to time by supplying suitable herbs for peoples' ailments, so it was a happy life on the whole. Our happiness was complete and our joy knew no bounds when our little Rosie was born, a beautiful child with her mother's lovely brown eyes and happy smile. We adored her and even my father came to visit and pay homage to his first grandchild. Robert's marriage had not yet produced the desired son, nor even a daughter (it was rumoured that his wife was too haughty and proud of her figure).

Our life now began to be a little easier. My poems were gradually becoming more popular. I would take them into the city inns and taverns and when the fiddlers had finished there would be a shout "Read as a poem, Jonathan". I was thus writing more and becoming more popular, even thinking about making a collection of the most popular poems and asking Mr Jenkins in the Haymarket to print them.

But meantime our little Rosie fell sick. She had a high fever and difficulty in breathing. The doctor couldn't give it a name and didn't know how to treat it but (if it was any consolation) many young children in the district were also suffering. With tears in her lovely eyes Mary said "Jonathan dear, what are we to do? We can't let Rosie suffer so. I've tried all the usual herbs for fever and they've not been any good. I'm tempted to try one of those secret recipes that my mother wrote down before she died. She would have been accused of witchcraft if people had known what she did. And I don't want to be accused of witchcraft either, but I must do something to try and help poor Rosie". So we reluctantly agreed to try one of the herbal mixtures that her mother had used secretly a generation ago. We thought we had no choice. Rosie was dying and nothing could harm her now. I never knew what the herb mixture was because Mary protected me from such dangerous knowledge, but whatever it was Rosie began to recover, slowly but, oh, so thankfully. Sadly, many other children died and Mary was troubled "If only I were allowed to help people more", she said.

There were severe penalties for being unorthodox in behaviour or ideas.

I had rejected the orthodox teachings of the Church when I left the seminary though I still attended the local church with increasing unease. There were people, however (they were called Quakers derisively) who had the courage to speak out against the hypocrisy and worldliness of the clergy and the hierarchical structure of the Church. Some were imprisoned for their views (one was actually in the jail at Westchester). Their ideas appealed to me, however, especially the idea that one could know the Holy Spirit within oneself without a priestly intermediary. This idea was revolutionary and dangerous but I felt it to be true to my own experience. Mary felt as I did, as we would often take Rosie and sit together under the beech tree beside the stream which inspired my best poems, and somehow we would feel a holy Presence within us, beyond words. There was no need for a priest or ritual, it was enough to feel the Presence within and allow oneself to be guided by it in one's daily life and conduct. So I came to feel impelled to seek out the local people who were friends of George Fox, the man in prison. They received me graciously and welcomed me in the meetings which were boldly in the open air, in the market square or other public place. They warned me of the danger but I offered to write tracts and broadsheets for them to publicise their message, as I felt more people would probably be interested. I knew there was widespread unease at the present state of the Church and several sects were beginning to spring up. So it was that I became a mouthpiece for the Quakers in Westchester, though I was never a preacher. It was an exhilarating time. I was kept busy, as so many people wanted to know about the Quakers' ideas. Sometimes a travelling preacher would come and hold a meeting outside the city; there was a favourite hillside with a natural amphitheatre which made a perfect meeting place. At those times huge crowds would assemble and I would hand out copies of my tracts. Mr Jenkins was happy to do the printing and people were usually happy to pay something towards the cost.

There was one especially memorable occasion when a famous travelling preacher came to our area. His name was Francis Howgill (the Quakers did not use titles as they were divisive and all human beings were of equal value before the Lord). He was a commanding figure, rugged, weatherworn with a ruddy complexion and broad practical hands. He explained that he was a farmer and had been 'seized of the Lord' and felt compelled to leave his farm and his family to become a preacher, to spread the good news of the immediate indwelling Spirit within each one. It was a perfect day in spring. The sun shone, the cold winds of winter had abated, the air was bright and clear so that we could see the whole valley down below, the city with its Castle on the hill and the old bridge spanning the river which shone like a silver ribbon in the sunlight. Francis Howgill stood on an outcrop of limestone which formed a natural pulpit on the hillside, and a goodly crowd of people assembled below him, some standing, some sitting on the outcrops, and some had even brought food with them. His voice carried well on the breeze and as he spoke I handed out tracts among the people noticing, however, that among the audience was the vicar of St. Peter's. He was an ominous looking figure, a tall cadaverous man whose long black coat and wide brimmed hat emphasised his leanness. His face was also long and lean, unsmiling and severe. I remembered his child was amongst the ones that had died of the strange illness, and wondered at his attitude towards the Quakers. I could hardly hope for a favourable response. And as Francis Howgill said "We meet together in the unity of the Spirit and in the bond of peace, treading down under our feet all reasoning about religion". I felt he had stirred up a fierce antagonism in Vicar West's heart.

I was not mistaken. It was full summer when the two men came to arrest me. Mary was indoors preparing our dinner, and I was with Rosie in our little garden where Mary and I had planted damask roses in memory of our first meeting. I was reading one of my stories to Rosie, a bright child who listened avidly with shining eyes to the improbable adventures I had created. The men were courteous enough but insisted on my going immediately with them to the court at the Castle. They also searched our house and took away my remaining printed tracts and even some of my poems. Mary was distraught, pleading with them, and Rosie cried and sobbed, clinging to me. "Don't leave us, Daddy" she cried, but I had to go, though trying as I went to assure Mary that as I'd done nothing wrong they wouldn't condemn me. But in my heart I didn't believe it. I knew that Quakers and others were imprisoned for no other reason than that they had dared to question ecclesiastical authority.

So I was taken to Westchester to the hilltop Castle, large, dominating the town, looking impregnable and forbidding. The great gates clanged shut behind me, sending shudders through me, but I tried not to show my anxiety and to remain calm. The courtroom was large and impressive with very solid thick stone walls and heavy dark furniture. The judge was a travelling judge, not from this area, and nobody mentioned his name. He sat high up on a raised bench with a table in front of him, reading my tracts. My accuser, Reverend West, stood to the right and related how he had watched me over many months and could produce other witnesses to my disloyal activities. "It is also well-known, Your Honour, that Quakers refuse to take the oath of allegiance". At this the judge gave a deep sigh as if in exasperation, and said "Six months in jail". So that was that. But it wasn't the end of the matter, rather the beginning. As there were so many cases before the court (mine was the last in that session) and so many sentenced to imprisonment, the jailer protested that he couldn't accommodate me - he already had far too many. So, after some consultation, they decided to send me to the old Castle 20 miles away up the river. It was semi-ruinous, they said, but the dungeon was still intact and it would suffice for six months. So I was driven away in a horse and cart - thankfully they didn't chain me - and on the way I learnt from the driver that my Mary had been accused of witchcraft by the Vicar West but had not been brought to court because he couldn't find any evidence, as no one had died from her herbal remedies. Thank God for that!

They were right about Bexby Castle and my heart sank at the sight. It was a crumbling ruin beside the river, but the underground dungeon was still intact and strongly built, though dark, damp and cold. They shut me in there with a little bread and a bowl of water, and left me. The contrast between this and our rose garden could not have been greater and I felt stifled in spite of the cold. I wondered who was going to look after me. There must be a jailer in Bexby, I supposed, even though there were normally no prisoners. I also wondered how Mary and Rosie would manage, and I hoped my parents would overcome their shame of having a son in prison and remember that their daughter-in-law and grandchild were innocent and needed help. I knew mother would be sympathetic as she really liked Mary, but she was powerless without father's approval.

How could I spend my time in the dark? I recited my old poems and composed new ones which I memorised against the day when I would be free and able to commit them to paper. And I walked up and down the dungeon to keep myself fit and warm - eight paces one way and six paces the other. So passed one day. I had no idea of night and day, of course, but slept at last from emotional exhaustion. When I awoke I drank the last of the water in the bowl, and hoped someone would come soon with something to eat. But the hours passed and no one came. I tried shouting but of course nobody could hear as I was underground, the walls and roof were thick and there was the noise of the river outside. Eventually I realised that I must have been forgotten. Obviously nobody in Bexby had been informed of my presence. And I was sentenced to six months! It would be impossible to survive so long. I would slowly starve. And how long can a man live without water? I had no means of calculating the time but very soon the hunger pains started, with the desperate desire for water. I began to feel weak and dizzy. The rats were a nuisance and I tried to get rid of them but they kept coming back. Soon I was too weak to fend them off and they started nibbling at my toes. After all, they were hungry too and I no longer cared what happened to my body. I tried to pray but my mind was numb. I was not made for martyrdom. This dreadful thirst, my lips and tongue feel swollen and I can't swallow. Mary! Rosie! We were so happy. The Vicar West destroyed it all and I hated him. I can picture him now in his long black coat, his face long and stern. But somehow I'm beginning to see him differently now. His face is not really so stern but very sad. He was heartbroken at the death of his only child, he felt that I was betraying God by rejecting the Church and all he believed in, and I think he really thought he was helping me to see the error of my ways. He acted out of sincere intention, as I did. So there is no cause for hatred and I can forgive him. But Jesus said "Love your enemies" and I can't love the Reverend West, that's asking too much. "You are never asked to do or be what you're not capable of". I'm seeing an angel now. I must be dying and having illusions. "It's no illusion. Look down and see the rats gnawing at your body. They are hungry and you have no further use for it. So, what did you learn in that life?" "I made the right choices this time. I married Mary and left the Church that I was not fitted for. I learnt to be sensitive to the indwelling divine Spirit, and at the end I learned forgiveness". "And what more do you still wish to learn?" "I want to be more aware of all this wonderful Spirit within and around me, but I know I have yet a long way to go. I also feel that in that life I was just beginning to realise a gift for leadership and I would like to develop that". "You shall be given that opportunity but it may not be as easy as you think".

Chapter 5

The sun was hot. I seized a moment to sneak out of the workshop and savour the warmth and freshness of the air outside. I didn't mind sweeping up the shavings and the sawdust although it was thirsty work and made me cough sometimes, and I enjoyed the company of the craftsmen and the sound of the saws and planes as they made the beautiful furniture which went to grace some of the best houses in Britain and the colonies. The owner, Mr Stansfield, was a master cabinet-maker though nowadays he worked mainly in the office and employed other master carpenters and apprentices to make the actual furniture. There weren't many of us, just James, William, John, Thomas the apprentice (who preferred to be called Redhead) and George a young lad who liked to come and watch us work with the option of becoming an apprentice.

My stolen moment was cut short, however, by the appearance of Mr Stansfield who had followed me. At first I thought he might be angry with me, though I'd always found him a fair and kind employer. But I realised he wasn't angry when he said to my surprise "I know you live with your widowed mother in the village, Muriel (forgive me for not addressing you as Miss Carter). I have known you for some years and know that you are a reliable worker. But what I'd like to know is, can you write a fair hand and are you good at figures? I need someone to help in the office and I would prefer to employ someone I know if possible". Well, this was a surprise. I didn't know what to say for a moment, he had so taken my breath away by defying the usual conventions of address. But I stood up straight and said "Yes, sir, I write a very fair hand and since father died I've looked after all the household affairs for mother and me. We are not rich and that has made me very careful in getting the figures right. I've seen how the wood comes in from the importers and how the furniture is packed for sending out with the carter and I'm sure I could help you, sir, if you will train me to do the work as you wish".

So it was agreed that I would start work in his office the next week.

Most of the men were pleased for me, especially the lad George who had taken to me from the beginning, though Redhead grumbled that he knew somebody else who would have done the job very well. Of course, when I told mother she was delighted. "So it was worthwhile, after all, your father teaching you all those things I didn't approve of at the time. I thought all that learning wasn't necessary for a girl, but you will earn more money and we shall live better in future. Mr Stansfield is a good employer and we should be grateful. Mind you do your best for him, it's a great honour. I don't know any other girls who are capable of working in an office, so learn all you can and work hard".

That was how I came to be that rarity, a lady Secretary. I found the work interesting and not too difficult. I enjoyed writing neat accounts in the big heavy ledger books and sending copies of the accounts to so many different places and fine houses, even sometimes to titled people. I saw too how, in spite of paying all our wages and the cost of the wood, there was a good profit for Mr Stansfield so that he himself could live in the biggest house in the village. He was a good teacher and I was a keen learner and we worked together very well, so I soon became quite efficient in the little office in the corner of the workshop. As time went on and I became more familiar with the running of the furniture making business I began to see where little improvements could make for more efficiency and greater rewards. At first I approached Mr Stansfield with some trepidation, as I feared he might think I was interfering and too forward, but he accepted my ideas graciously. "Don't hesitate, Muriel, if you can think of ways of improving the business, just come to me at any time and we'll discuss them". So it happened that, a few months later, I had an idea to present to him. "We haven't time to discuss it here", he said, "The dining table and chairs for Alston Hall are due to be sent out and the accounts are not yet ready. So attend to that urgently. His Lordship is impatient as he is expecting important guests, and he's a good customer. Perhaps it would be best if you come to the Manor after work; you'd have more time to explain your ideas and we could discuss them at leisure."

I had seen the outside of his house, naturally, as it was at the top of the village street, looking down the hill at our modest cottages which lined the street, down to the little bridge over the river below. People said it was a picturesque village and I agreed it was a very pleasant place to live and work, as it was friendly and only a short step to the workshop beside the bridge. But I'd always admired Mr Stansfield's house, Parton Manor, the warm glow of its rich red sandstone, and the Doric columns at the front making it look so grand. And grand it was, with so many big windows compared to our little cottages. The Manor was relatively new, having been rebuilt by Mr Stansfield's father, the founder of the business. But there was nobody to continue the tradition as Mr Stansfield's wife and son had died in childbirth many years ago and now he was a lonely widower considerably older than me though still attractive in spite of his stooping shoulders and shy manner. Perhaps it was his shyness that made him seem attractive and different from the other men I had met. I'd always wanted to see inside the Manor but Mr Stansfield's shyness made him unsociable; the county people were not invited and it was only the local vicar and Doris, the daily housekeeper, who had access to the intimacy of the interior. Doris had reported "big rooms, beautiful furniture all of the best mahogany, soft rugs, crystal chandeliers and candlesticks, fine silver, fireplaces even in the bedrooms though these were never lit as he didn't have guests. He is easy to look after and has simple tastes for himself but likes to surround himself with beautiful things."

So I was very excited at the prospect of actually being a guest at the Manor, even though it was part of my work and not a social call. Mr Stansfield received me very graciously in his study, after Doris had opened the ornately panelled front door to me and led me through a large hall to the back of the house. The study was an austere room, square, lined with books on three sides, with a pretty plaster ceiling and glazed doors leading to a walled garden which was receiving the evening sunlight. "Please sit down, Muriel. Doris shall bring us some tea and we can talk about your ideas". Tea! I'd never tasted tea and wondered if I should like it. I was becoming more and more nervous, but I chose a chair by the window, took a deep breath, sat up straight and told him how I thought he could reduce his costs and at the same time increase production. "As it is now, Sir, the workshop gets so crowded with finished pieces of furniture waiting to be delivered that it is difficult to move around and work on the new pieces. The men complain they haven't room to work properly and we have to pay somebody to keep moving pieces from one place to another. Do you think it would help if we build a shed at the entrance, by the bridge - there's room enough - to put the new furniture in, away from the dust and easier for the carter to pick up when he comes. Being near the entrance and the road over the bridge, people travelling from Yorkshire down to Lancaster would see our furniture and perhaps stop to order a piece." Mr Stansfield fingered the silver buttons on his coat, looked thoughtful but said nothing. I went on "And another thing, Sir, our young lad George is saying he'd like to go to Lancaster to be apprenticed to Mr Gillow. He's a promising lad and could do better in a larger establishment and I think we shouldn't hold him back. His father has a cousin in Lancaster who could give him accommodation".

I waited anxiously for Mr Stansfield's answer. Would he think me too impertinent and too forward? After all, I was only an employee and a woman. Why should he listen to me?

Mr Stansfield was looking fixedly out of the window, past me to where the setting sun was casting long shadows over the garden; he was frowning, deep in thought, but after what seemed to me an uncomfortable silence he spoke. "I think you have good ideas, Muriel, sensible and forward-looking. I think we should co-operate more. I'm getting old and times are changing. I believe that there are experiments going on with some sort of machinery for the textile trade and it may be they'll invent machinery for our trade in the future. I'm too old and set in my ways. The old family firm needs new blood if it is to continue and I have no son unfortunately nor even any nephews". At this he paused, looking at me very intently. Then he braced himself, took a deep breath and said "I've known you for many years now, Muriel, and you seem to me to represent the future. You have the firm's welfare at heart, you have a good head on your shoulders, a natural talent for business and we work together very well. I have been thinking of this for a long time and my regard for you has steadily grown. Would you consider a business partnership, Muriel? If you could consider this I would seriously offer you marriage, to avoid any embarrassment for you. I hope I have not given you any cause to distrust me. My intentions are honourable. I have a genuine regard and great respect for you; there may not be love between us but a partnership based on mutual respect is not dishonourable. I don't expect your answer today but will you please agree to think about it, talk it over with your mother and give me your answer when you are ready".

The precious tea and the beautiful Meissen cups lay untouched. The atmosphere of the room had become highly charged though not with emotion - with suppressed emotion perhaps. So I left the Manor with my head spinning and thoughts chasing each other in my mind. I liked Mr Stansfield and we got on very well during the working hours together, but marriage? What a wonderful thing it would be if I could be mistress of the Manor and a partner in the business! I thought of the fine paintings and the beautiful furniture in those splendid rooms. I'd only seen one room but my imagination pictured the splendour of the withdrawing room, the dinner parties one could have in the dining-room. And perhaps I could have a servant or two instead of Doris who was getting old. My imagination knew no bounds, as I mentally thought of new fabrics in lighter colours for the window draperies, and how an elegant vase with a colourful spray of flowers would look well on the Italian marquetry commode. And then the doubts came. Was I really capable of running a business, which it would come to in the end? And was I fitted by birth and upbringing to be mistress of a large house? And the vital question, could I live with a man I didn't love, an older man who would eventually need me to look after him?

Mother was not very helpful. She was of a similar age to Mr Stansfield and understood his needs and his motives, she said, but I must make my own decision. Few women had such an opportunity, I knew, and the questions and arguments for and against buzzed in my head incessantly the next few days, as Mr Stansfield and I went about our normal business, trying to ignore the heavy atmosphere between us. So I hovered in an agony of indecision between avarice and self-doubt, swinging first one way and then the other. I dare not discuss it with my friends as I knew they would say "marry him and enjoy your good luck" though I think Evelyn would be the cautious one; she believed a woman should marry for love, have children and stay at home (which, I had to admit, was the normal attitude of society). She disapproved even when I became the sweeper at the factory, though she did admit it was an economic necessity for mother and me. But after all it was my life and my decision, and after days and nights of oscillation I decided to accept Mr Stansfield's offer (by this time I discovered his name was Philip). When I told him he was quite silent for a moment and then took my hand and with great gentleness and courtesy kissed it and said "You do me a great honour, my dear, and I will do my best to be a good husband to you." His humility touched me greatly and brought tears to my eyes. I felt mean, as I was only marrying him for position, power and wealth, but I replied, and meant it, that although I couldn't give him love I would be a faithful wife and helpmate. So a wedding was arranged for later that summer in the local parish church. The vicar was somewhat disapproving when we told him of our decision. He was an old friend of Philip's and perhaps he thought he would not be invited to the Manor so often in the future, but I assured him I intended to entertain and hoped he would become my friend too. This was an early attempt on my part to acquire the condescending manner of the gentry!

Meantime, George had departed for Lancaster, very thrilled at having greater scope to develop his talents, and the men had made a start on building the shed by the entrance. I asked them to make it as attractive as possible, to be a showroom for our furniture. I had plans in my head to add some of the new fabrics from the Lancashire weavers, but that would come later.

The wedding was a quiet affair but I carried myself proudly in a gown of green silk, the full sleeves decorated with exquisite lace, and Philip looked so noble and kind, resplendent in a new wig and a long green velvet coat with silver buttons and lace cuffs. My mother cried of course, though I think they were tears of joy; she knew she would be a frequent visitor at the Manor. The local people had differing attitudes, I knew; the younger ones were mostly envious, the older ones either thinking it a suitable arrangement or strongly disapproving of a local girl presuming to become the lady of the Manor. They were all invited to the Manor for the wedding breakfast, however, and I'm sure they all avidly eyed the splendours of my new home.

So my life as Mrs Stansfield began. Philip introduced me to the traders who supplied us with timber and to the shippers who transported the furniture to clients in the colonies. Often they were the same people, trading in imports and exports from the port of Sunderland at the mouth of Lancaster's river. At first they were reluctant to deal with a woman, and one or two thought that, being a woman, I could be cheated. But I soon proved my competence and asserted my authority and relations with all our traders became amicable. As time went on, however, I was tempted to use the new docks in the developing port of Liverpool as it seemed to me to be the port of the future. But the carters grumbled about the distance and the roads; the old Roman roads were in a very bad state and the new turnpikes were too expensive. Although I was keen to keep the business in the forefront of fashion and accepting of new ideas I decided to continue trading with Sunderland. But I made agreements with several textile workers in Lancashire; they were excellent spinners and weavers and could send their goods by mule over the moors quite cheaply. So our new shed at the entrance became an attractive shop, where we did good trade with the passing carriages of the gentry. And as our business expanded, so we eventually had to extend our premises at the rear and take on more craftsmen. I hoped George would come back to us when he finished his apprenticeship but he was more ambitious and went on to London. We never heard from him again but hoped he was successful. It's not easy to be successful in London.

So the years passed. The business was flourishing and the Manor never looked so splendid, with new draperies, silver tableware and candelabra with new wax candles, and beautiful new porcelain from Sevres for the tea which I now drank quite frequently. But Philip was becoming more feeble, a thin spare figure, stooping and walking with a stick, but as kind and gentle as ever. And I had over the years come to feel an increasing regard for him; I couldn't call it love but it was a comfortable relationship, especially after our son was born, Peter, named after Philip's father. I really believe that Philip loved me in a selfless sort of way. He never criticised my social mistakes (and I made many in the early days of our marriage) but accepted me as I was. This made me feel secure, perhaps even content, though I wouldn't call it happiness. I certainly fulfilled my marriage vows and cared for Philip, making sure he had every comfort and every kind of medication that would help him to walk more easily. He took great pride in Peter, hoping he would continue the business for the third generation but Peter had inherited my self-will and assertiveness and had chosen to adventure abroad. So, although it was a disappointment to us, we accepted his decision and bade him farewell as he embarked at Liverpool for the Grand Tour.

As Philip grew feebler I became gradually in sole charge of the business, which was steadily expanding. I really enjoyed running the business and felt proud that I was so successful. Mr Atkins, our main export agent, said one day that I was "every bit as good as a man". He meant it as a compliment so I accepted it as such, though I felt I was only fulfilling my natural abilities. Mr Atkins would have approved of my womanly attributes too, I think, as I spent more time with Philip; he rarely visited the factory now and we would spend time together in the morning room which was pleasantly furnished in blue and gold, and received the morning light at the front of the house. Or, on a fine day, we would sit in the garden beside the little pool and fountain I had installed. He enjoyed these times we had together and I also enjoyed his company; his conversation was always interesting because of his superior education and he had an innate wisdom which I admired and envied. But the day came when I returned from the factory to find him sitting in his favourite chair asleep, as I thought, but it was his final sleep. I was glad that he'd had no pain and no protracted illness. My Philip, whom I'd come to rely on for support and understanding. What was I going to do without him? I should have been kinder. He was so good to me, what had I given him in return? Such thoughts tormented me for many months but the business had to be attended to and life had to continue. I sent word to Peter but he was too far away to return for the funeral. I had hoped that the news of his father's death would make him decide to return and enter the business after all. He had other ideas, however, and wrote that he was collecting curios, antiques and local craft work on his travels, would shortly be sending home crates of goods and would return later to set up a shop dealing in antiques and curios. So I resigned myself to being the last Stansfield of 'Stansfield Furniture'. It was very sad after so many years of dedicated effort, but my heart was no longer in it. I was not young any more and felt very tired at times. There wasn't any incentive to make an effort and I spent more time at home. The Manor was very dear to me; it held happy memories and I still enjoyed its beauty and its comforts. I employed Agnes, the daughter of my old friend Evelyn, to look after the housekeeping and I spent my days quietly, rarely venturing farther than the village. Peter's crates had arrived and the contents added to our display at the factory entrance, which had by now become a large and attractive shop. It was into this tranquility that the news came as a shattering blow. Peter had been on his way home, crossing France, and had got caught up in riots in Paris, serious revolutionary riots, which had taken his life. Many others had been killed and the bodies hastily buried, they said. I could not go to Paris to find his body and I had no idea where he had been laid. My poor Peter. Such high hopes for a brilliant life, all for nothing. And now I had really nothing. There was nobody left who mattered to me, and the beautiful home which I cherished seemed to have no attraction any more - the house, the garden, furnishings, all the silks and silver, all were simply objects of no value to me, as if everything had turned to dust and ashes. "What have I got to live for?" was the question I often asked myself. But there was no answer.

Putting Redhead, now the most senior craftsman, in charge of the factory I had become completely withdrawn from life. Now I am very old and weary, with no wish to live and afraid to die. My life is wasted again. Why do I think 'again'? I seem to have vague memories that I can't quite grasp. The present is fading, I can't see the room, everything is becoming a long way away. But I'm remembering again, that wonderful Light is coming back. Or I'm coming back to the Light.

What does it mean? "It means you are here to assess your life, consider your achievements and your unfulfilled aims, and think about what you need to do in the future to bring you closer to your ambition". My ambition? My aims? I never thought about it. "We will help you think about it". Who are these 'we'? I see nobody, but seem to be aware of presences around me; I hear no sound and yet the voice is clear. It speaks to my soul, my innermost being, and tells me that I made the same mistake as before. I have chosen material things instead of love. I used my organising talent for the business and for the acquisition of wealth, and it came to dominate my life. I gave compassion and caring to Philip and Peter, but I could have given more love. My motives in marrying Philip were wrong, I think it was right to marry him but he needed me to care for him for his own sake rather than for his possessions. If only I'd let Philip teach me about selfless love! I see now how wrong I was, how I fell short of what I could have been. How can I ever atone for these mistakes? "If you really desire to learn unconditional love you will be given that opportunity again in a future incarnation. Meantime, rest here in this beautiful garden and learn from the Masters.

Your longing for the Light and for Love will not ever leave you, and you have yet many lessons to learn."

Chapter 6

The sun was hot. The wafer-thin sandwiches were curling up in the orangery behind Lady Dalmichael, as she stood on the terrace making her speech to the garden party guests assembled on the lawns below. "Ladies and gentlemen", she began, "I'm sure you all know why you have been invited to Dalmichael Hall. I know you are all deeply interested in the welfare of our black brothers in Africa and wish to bring them the benefits of civilisation and Christian morals. But you are here today especially to meet the gentleman who is going out himself to Africa, to bring these benefits in person to the Africans, Mr Thomas Brooks". Here she paused for applause, while I eyed the sandwiches. "Mr Brooks is highly qualified for the task", she went on, "He is an experienced doctor of sound morals, and is young and healthy enough to withstand the undoubted rigours of the task. He will mingle among you as you enjoy our hospitality and he is willing to answer your questions to enable you to give most generously and confidently to the expedition. He will, of course, be taking a supply of Bibles with him. So please enjoy the beautiful day in the garden and the company of Mr Brooks. Your donations may be placed in the oak box in the orangery". Thus having spoken, Lady Dalmichael threw me to the lions. I had no stomach for this sort of elegant gathering. The ladies, I suspected, were eyeing one another's gowns to see which was most fashionable. The older ones or more conservative ones still wore the graceful and simple high-waisted dress which I admired, but some of the younger ones had burst out in crinolines of all kinds and colours with flounces, frills and parasols. Such a lot of silly women. And the men accompanying the women, unwillingly I suspected, and merely there to provide the money to buy such a prestigious social occasion, were as uncomfortable as I in formal day wear in the heat. But such things had to be endured.

I had been practising medicine in Westchester hospital for a few years but felt restless as if I needed to travel, to experience foreign adventures. I was young and healthy, as Lady Dalmichael had said and, although I was considered to be an eligible bachelor and all the dowagers at the garden party were no doubt casting calculating eyes on me, I was less interested in marriage than in travel. In order to achieve this ambition, I didn't mind taking a few Bibles if that would finance the adventure. Africa was an exciting prospect, an unknown continent for the most part, and I felt confident that, as a doctor, I could earn my passage wherever I went. So I mingled with the county elite, made polite and flattering remarks as required, admired the rose garden, commented on the smooth texture of the lawns and how noble the Hall looked above the balustraded terrace, its large sash windows glinting in the sunlight.

Lady Dalmichael's was the last of such garden parties I had to endure that summer, but there was still the hurdle of the interview with the Negro Conversion Society's advisory council. I was relying on them for the major part of my finance and for contacts in Africa, but I didn't look forward to what I expected would be a lengthy interrogation of my motives, background and morals. In the event it was better than I expected. At the end of the interview the chairman of the council said he had known my father (both my parents had died some years before) and was confident of my suitability for the work. In addition he said, "Your father was the son of an old friend of mine and I held him in high regard and trust that his son is worthy of this important work of bringing the Christian faith and civilised ways to the heathen. But to aid you in this work - you are after all inexperienced - you will have an assistant, a younger man of very serious intent and enthusiasm. His name is John Eastwood and he is the nephew of our president. So I can rely on you to look after him, and he in turn will be a help to you as he has been studying medicine these last three years in Edinburgh and has a firm Christian faith. We are pleased to support such a fine pair of medical men, and we are confident that your spiritual efforts will be richly blessed. A crate of Bibles will be sent to Liverpool to await your embarkation. Your itinerary, provided by an experienced trader in Africa, will be forwarded to you within a few days, together with the formal notice of your appointment".

I quite welcomed the idea of an assistant but wish I had been consulted. "What if this John Eastwood and I are incompatible and unable to work harmoniously together? But if he has such enthusiasm for the Christian faith perhaps I can put him in charge of the Bibles and their distribution. Those earnest men on the council no doubt feel they are doing the Lord's work but I've no time or patience for interfering in other people's beliefs". These thoughts were going through my mind as I spent the next few weeks in feverish activity, collecting and buying tropical kit and suitable equipment and medical supplies. This was a task I had to accomplish alone, as John Eastwood lived in London, was making his purchases there and would join me in Liverpool when the clipper arrived.

So the momentous day came when we met and embarked together on the 'Indian Isles', a fast three-masted clipper that had just arrived from Jamaica with rum and tobacco and could then sail on with iron and cloth goods for Africa. John was a fresh-faced young man with innocent blue eyes and a helpless appealing look about him. My first impression was not favourable but he soon proved his worth by very efficiently organising the storage of our crates and personal effects. We shared accommodation with the crew and soon showed ourselves to be bad sailors as we entered the open sea and met a westerly gale. We daren't use our precious medical supplies on ourselves, so suffered until we became accustomed to the ship's movement.

To us the journey seemed endless, but the sailors said it was a fast crossing with a favourable wind and at length we dropped anchor on the coast of Africa near the town of Lagos which was the main trading port used by the clipper's captain. As we came ashore we noticed the negro slaves waiting to be shipped to the Plantations. John was immediately appalled by the sight and broke out, "How can so many hundreds of men and women be packed into that ship we have just disembarked from? They will never survive the conditions and the ship isn't big enough to carry all the people, food and water at the same time". But I knew there was a sound reason for this. "You see, John, it's a very uncertain trade. Now that the traders can't land slaves in Britain they have to go all the way across the Atlantic to America to sell them. So the cost has risen and the price has dropped due to lower demand, as America will probably follow Britain's lead, and so the captains have to carry as many as possible to allow for wastage. Those who survive will be the stronger ones and will fetch a better price". John was not convinced. "I still think one shouldn't treat people like that. They may be black and heathen and not much better than animals but they are children of the Lord and it is our duty to care for them and teach them". "You are too idealistic, John", I replied, "My father had a couple of slaves. They worked well, but only when he was watching them, and when he died and I had to clear up his affairs I got rid of them. They are supposed to be free now anyway, so they can find their own place to live and work, and perhaps feel some gratitude for what my father did for them. I remember him saying they didn't cost much, and I suppose the British economy will suffer now that we shall have to pay higher wages for white people to do the work". However, even I was somewhat astonished to see the negroes herded into a sort of secure wire cage and guarded by men with guns.

But it was none of our business, and we proceeded to collect our belongings on the shore and make the acquaintance of the trader who had awaited our arrival and had organised oxcart transport and porters for our journey into the interior. We planned to join the river Niger at Jebba, proceed down it to Lokoja and then head for the upland regions of the river Benue. The rivers were the main thoroughfare, so we proceeded from village to village following this route, though many times we had to take to the forest to avoid rapids and waterfalls; in such cases the porters simply carried the flimsy looking canoes and their contents on their shoulders. "You know, John", I said one day as we followed the negroes along the forest trail, stumbling over roots and trailing vines, "These fellows are quite different in their own country. At home the negroes are lazy and sullen, here they are fine upstanding figures, confident of where they are going and how to live in this hell of a country and diabolical climate. Here we are the weaklings, bathed in sweat from morning until night, plagued by insects of every kind, and ready to rest at any opportunity". The trader, Jim Baker, had acquired enough of the native languages (and there were many) to understand them and John was also a good learner, so we were able to profit by the negroes' experience of these rivers. Also, our Jim Baker was not a dealer in slaves, so the natives were more inclined to trust us the further we penetrated into the interior. John was very practical and insisted on giving out Bibles at each village where we were given hospitality. At least it lightened the load to be carried. And John proved to have an affinity with pregnant women, and delivered several babies on the way. There seemed to be no shortage of babies and, as in England, many apparently died young or if they survived they were required to work. I treated wounds of many kinds, caused by accidents in the forest, encounters with wild animals or sometimes a personal quarrel.

So we progressed through dense jungle, slowly and painfully over many weeks, treating what maladies we could and trading cloth, brightly coloured glass beads and other trinkets in exchange for hospitality. Jim Baker was anxious, however, to reach the upland region towards the mountains, where he said there was a tribe that fashioned strange carvings out of ivory, and he wished to acquire some to take back to England. John said "Why not make that village our final stop, too. They sound to be a more sophisticated people and we may be happier with them. Besides, Jim will be returning with the porters to the coast, and we can't go further on our own. Don't you agree, Mr Brooks?" I did agree but resented his assuming to take charge, which is why I insisted on his addressing me formally as Mr Brooks. I felt I had to assert my authority and not let our standards slip just because we were away from civilisation.

The heat became less intense as we followed the river through the forest to the hill country, though the plagues of insects didn't seem to lessen and the air was just as humid. But at last we came to a large clearing and the village which was to be our home for an indefinite future. Several of the men came out to meet us, no doubt to assess what kind of whites we were and what out purpose was. They were tall men, well built and strong looking, a little suspicious but friendly enough. We on our part showed by sign language that we had friendly intentions. Jim Baker explained our mission and the black porters were happy to fraternise with the local men. Although of different tribes they were accustomed to meet whenever any of the traders penetrated so far inland in their direction.

So, after a short rest, Jim Baker and the porters departed for the coast again and we were left to settle into our new home. We chose an open spot in the village and organised some of the local men to build us a hut of timber with a roof of grasses and vines. It was to have two rooms, one for our surgery and the other our living quarters. This was soon accomplished, the men being expert at the task as huts were constantly being reviewed after damage or destruction by insects or the heavy rains. John wanted to build a church as well but I said that could wait. Really, I was getting tired of John always making suggestions and assuming he knew what was needed. I had to assert my authority and keep him in his place. Women seemed to be naturally attracted to him - it must have been his 'little boy' look of helpless innocence - so I let him deal with the women of the tribe while I attended to the problems of the men. It took a while before they would trust us, however, as, while they had met white traders before they had never met white doctors. They had never seen a stethoscope or thermometer, for instance, and they were afraid we were going to harm them. So I was obliged to enlist the help of the local medicine woman, whom they trusted completely. I called her Maria because she had a Madonna-like oval face and beautiful brown eyes and a tender smile - and besides, I couldn't pronounce her real name. She accepted us and welcomed the new knowledge we brought, but indicated that her own ways of treating patients were equally valid and we should accept her help on her terms. I was quite willing to do this but John protested with horror "We can't work with a witch doctor. Witches are illegal in England and against Biblical teaching. It would be wicked to co-operate with the devil". But his women patients insisted they wanted Maria to help with her herbs, magic incantations and healing hands, so he had to give in with a bad grace. Actually, I found Maria helpful, particularly when I needed to relieve pain or lessen the painful effect of an operation. I had heard that more effective and safer methods of controlling pain were being developed but we had nothing here but simple herbs, even our ether was finished. Maria seemed able to soothe and relax the patients more effectively than either John or me, so I was thankful for the help, witch or not, and I wrote a report on our experiences, though I don't know if it was ever published.

Jim Baker was right about the ivory carvings. They were intricate and strange but they appealed to me. I thought them beautiful in an unusual sort of way, but John dismissed them as 'heathen idols'. He had achieved his ambition and built a church, so he enjoyed officiating there on Sundays. I think the natives enjoyed the dressing up and the singing but I doubt if they understood much about the Bible stories and none of them wished to be baptised as Christians. As I said to John "They also have a God. Is it the same God as ours with a different name or are there several Gods? And what about Adam and Eve? If we are all descended from them, how did we come to have different colours? Some of their descendants who settled in hot countries must have developed a different kind of darker skin, while others in cold countries went paler and became white. But that must have taken much longer than the Biblical scholars say humanity has lived on earth. I don't understand the clever scholars and keep my thoughts to myself as a rule. But here there is nobody to criticise or denounce me. You can think what you like, John, and I'll think my own thoughts."

Theology was not the only thing that divided us, and as time went on we grew increasingly apart. We worked together but otherwise had little in common, and I became more and more irritated by him, even actively disliking him and resenting his presence. Also, I must admit, I was jealous of his popularity with the women patients.

My dislike of John was justified eventually, when Jim Baker returned for more ivory carvings, bringing with him brightly coloured cloth and even some soft toys for the children. He brought us letters from the Negro Conversion Society which informed us that they could not any longer support us as we had made no converts to Christianity and the civilising work was being adequately carried out by traders. They believed it was not necessary to equip negroes with medicines. Jim also brought news of developments in anaesthetics and Darwin's new theory of evolution. For my ears only he brought news from London of John's past and the reason why he was here. Apparently his appealing looks had attracted women in London, too, and he'd made a girl pregnant and, in attempting an abortion, the girl had died. His father was a prominent figure in the Church and couldn't allow a scandal, so he took advantage of the Society's connection to ship him as far away as possible.

So that explained quite a lot, his excessive orthodoxy in religion, his desire to 'redeem' the heathen, and his hypocrisy. My dislike for him grew week by week, as we were forced to be together in that damned climate. I became more and more irritable and critical, and could scarcely contain my contempt for John; it was obvious I must try to protect the local women from him. There were already more than enough babies. I didn't want to see any mixed-race ones. I hinted a little of my fears to Maria and she smiled her wise, calm smile and assured me the women knew the sort of man he was - attractive but not to be trusted. And they considered me trustworthy but unattractive, was her unsolicited remark. I didn't know whether to be flattered or insulted and decided to ignore the remark. I could have said, but didn't, that I had increasing respect for her, and something even approaching friendship. It had never occurred to me before that I could possibly feel friendship for a black person, a negro, but working with Maria had changed me in some away. Perhaps it was this diabolical climate, I thought, sapping one's energy and draining away one's will with the sweat.

John also was feeling the effect of our long exposure to the humidity. He appeared listless and complained of pain. As the pain grew worse in spite of all our efforts he himself diagnosed the pain as appendicitis and asked me to remove the offending part. Although great strides had been made in anaesthetics since we had left England, there was nothing here to help him as our former ether stocks were depleted, and Maria's herbs and incantations would hardly prepare him for surgery. So he had to endure the surgery with Maria holding his hand and me holding the knife. I held the scalpel poised to open him up and felt an extraordinary passion of hatred which momentarily dominated me. I met Maria's eyes, calm, steady, penetrating, as if she knew my thoughts - and somehow the moment passed and I performed the operation, removed a large inflamed vermiform appendix and stitched him up, feeling drained of all emotion except horror at the iniquity of my thoughts.

After that episode our relationship gradually improved, mainly due to my changed attitude, I must admit. I saw how I had let prejudice build up in me until I had a completely distorted opinion of John. I could see him now as a man who was trying in the best way he knew to atone for his error he made when much younger. I would in future try not to pass judgement on people, though I'm afraid I very often failed in this resolve.

John recovered, thankfully, and seemed reconciled to live amongst Negroes. His attitude softened and he was less dogmatic about his religion, even prepared to use the local deities in his sermons as expressions of Christian virtues, when appropriate.

But as John's health improved mine deteriorated. I had always found the humidity very debilitating and after so long suffering and trying in vain to adapt to the climate and conditions my body was giving way to extreme lethargy. It was not surprising, therefore, that I finally fell victim to the dreaded malaria fever, for which there was as yet no treatment or cure. John and Maria nursed me devotedly through several bouts of violent shivers and hot sweats, and the absolute exhaustion. Maria's hand was the only help available, but it was always soothing and calming even in the worst attacks. At these times John had to act as the sole doctor for the area, which kept him very busy as natives trekked through the forest and down the river to receive the white man's help. He was training Maria to act as a nurse to perform simple medical tasks, which was a great change of attitude on his part and which I approved wholeheartedly. I felt there would inevitably come a time when Negroes must receive medical training and become competent doctors and nurses, able to treat the diseases common among their own populations. Maria was a beginning; she was able to combine her own traditions with ours, which I felt was an advantage.

When well, I worked as hard as ever, but I couldn't withstand the bouts of malaria for long. I became ever weaker and began to suffer hallucinations. "John is forgiving me for wanting to kill him. How did he know? Maria's eyes, so wise, so understanding. I need her forgiveness too. I judged everybody - John, the ladies of the garden parties, the council members, the Negroes, and never looked for their good qualities. I wanted adventure but couldn't accept the accompanying difficulties. My life was a failure and now I see my body lying in that African hut, but I'm surrounded by crowds of people. I don't understand. If I'm dead, then they must be dead and yet they have bodies". "You are being given a dying vision of people of all shades of pigmented skin from palest white to darkest black. All are as you, representations of the Godhead learning to adapt the attributes of Godhead - love, compassion, peace, joy - to the conditions of a tiny star you call Earth. So you were right. There are many Gods and the One God has many names including yours, Thomas. Can you remember this when next you visit Earth, Thomas?". "This is too awesome a thought. I need time to think about it and absorb it. But it does explain the strange feelings and the yearnings I've had, the sort of longing for the divine, insatiable, inexplicable longing, even when I've been arrogant, selfish and domineering and in spite of all my harsh and cruel thoughts and opinions. If I'm given more time and if I'm given your help (whoever, whatever you are) then perhaps I shall remember more of this wonderful experience". "I am always with you in your innermost being, Thomas. You need only to be still, and listen."

PART TWO

Early years.

Waaaha! Here we go again, slapped on the bottom, dunked in water, manhandled. I wonder what I'm here for this time? I didn't want to be born. I was happy where I was.

Waaaha! A brass band at a christening, what are they thinking of? I don't like noise and I wish they would go away.
Waaaha! And now they've started on the organ. I DON'T LIKE NOISE. What are they trying to do to me? I wish they'd be quiet and let me think. There's something I need to remember.

My parents were keen churchgoers (Non-conformists) and I was taken with them to church from babyhood. I remember cuddling under mother's arm and being given a sweet to keep me quiet during the sermon, but my parents didn't realise the sweet wasn't needed as I spent the sermon time talking with Jesus, often asking him why grown-ups didn't behave like it said in the Gospels. For the same reason I was always willing to go to bed, to commune with Jesus, who was my childhood 'phantom friend'. Our conversation was always two-way. I would, in a childish way, ask guidance for my daily life and behaviour, and Jesus would tell me what he wanted me to do and be. There was one particularly agonising problem I remember. "Which do I love most, my parents or God?" God was a remote figure, the all-powerful Creator and I didn't have a personal relationship with him as I had with Jesus, but after long and earnest discussion with Jesus I decided I loved God best. Maybe it was partly because I was an only child that I never had any problem of loneliness; I learnt very early in life to 'go within' for spiritual sustenance. But I did want a baby sister to care for. My parents told me I couldn't have one, though I was too young to understand the reason (my mother was over forty when I was born). So, although I was more interested in building with meccano I had a life-sized doll and was quite sure that God would be able to breathe life into her for me. So I prayed very hard and had complete faith, running downstairs in the morning to be ready to feed and change her. I don't remember how many days this happened until at last I came to terms with the fact that God doesn't necessarily answer prayers in the way we expect.

Another experience came a little later. My little school friend Joan had a baby sister whom we used to wheel in her pram to the Park on Saturdays. The baby died, however, and for some reason the family (Joan was the youngest of 12 children) invited me to view the body at their house. There, in its little coffin was what seemed to me to be a wax doll. That wasn't the baby we'd cared for and played with, and I wondered why all the grown-ups were so upset - didn't they know she'd gone to live with Jesus? This literal acceptance of the Gospels is characteristic of childhood of course. Another episode was with another primary school friend (we were 'infants' in those days); we all lived in a poor neighbourhood near the fish docks in Hull and the school was in the next street to my home. My friend, as well as being poor, had habits I didn't like very much, she picked her nose and then wiped her fingers in my long hair for one thing but she was my friend. Mother always kept me clean (though I suffered from periodic fine-tooth combing for nits) and well-clothed as she was a professional dressmaker, but I was the only child in my class with shoes, I remember. There was one winter's day of heavy rain and cold wind, and my little friend, who lived farther from the school than I did, had no coat as well as no shoes. So I gave her my coat. It seemed the obvious thing to do. I knew my mother could make me another one, as my clothes were made from remnants left over from her adult dress making orders, but she wasn't at all happy at my action and I was forbidden to have anything to do with my friend in the future. She came from a very undesirable family, they said.

Another primary school episode involved me using the remnants myself. I had the idea to make up a 'lucky bag' containing a remnant of material, a needle and some thread, and sell the bags at a penny to my classmates for making doll's clothes. This became very popular and I made a good profit, to such an extent that my mother began to think I'd make a good businesswoman. At that time - I was nine and she was fifty and probably suffering from the menopause - she asked me to consider seriously if I wanted to carry on her business after I left school, which would have been after five years. A very serious decision for a nine-year-old to make, but I had a vision of myself in the future as a successful and rich businesswoman, running a chain of shops, and I didn't like myself. So I told mother I wanted to stay as long as possible at school, and she thereupon decided to retire and move to the West Coast where she had inherited a house.

Mother had always been the breadwinner as father had lost two fingers in his right hand in a lathe during the First World War, there was no compensation and no dole and no work for engineers in the depression years of my childhood. Father was very important to me, though, as he was always at home in the back room while mother attended to the shop in the front room. It was father who taught me to read (and recite the alphabet backwards!) before going to school. He also talked to me about his thoughts on philosophy from his reading of the three books we possessed Maeterlinck, Emerson and Tupper. In fact, he was such a disciple of Emerson that mother always called him Waldo instead of his given name of William. Philosophical concepts were often discussed and argued about, mother being the sceptical one, but apparently I once loftily observed "I think my own thinks!"

I must have been a very difficult child, self opinionated and self-sufficient. One episode which must have been particularly trying for my gentle pacifist father was an occasion when I had been especially objectionable and he gave me a slap. Apparently I looked at him reproachfully and said "Fancy, a great big man like you hitting a little girl like me". That was the first and only time I got slapped but I must often have driven my parents' patience to the limit as they often said "Nobody will ever love you, you are unlovable". This was probably said in a fit of extreme exasperation but it cut deep and lasted for most of my life. I became shy and even more dependent on my inward resources, afraid to offer friendship because I was sure it would be rejected, suffering for many years from low self-esteem and under-valuing myself and my capabilities. I now realise that a great many people suffer the same lack of self-esteem which holds them back from developing their full potential, and through my own experience I have learnt to give others encouragement and assurances of support and love.

Secondary school days.

My years at secondary school were not very memorable. I was already beginning to forget those pre- birth memories. I learned to love being by the sea and spent hours on the beach just absorbing the sounds, the movement and the changing colours of the sea and the sky. I wrote poetry. I attempted to make friends but found my shyness was a barrier and nobody else seemed to share my interest in nature. By that time other girls were beginning to be interested in boys, which I found a very boring topic. I was judgmental, greedy, ridiculed and rejected. I was no good at games, being large, clumsy and very fat (I weighed 14 stone by the time I was 14) and as I couldn't run I was made a team leader. But I was no good at that either as I didn't care which team won and cheered them all indiscriminately. I was still attending church and became a Sunday School teacher for a while, but eventually came to the teenage period of rebellion. I didn't believe in God any more, or at least I persuaded myself I didn't believe but I really think I felt it was my duty to doubt. But doubt I did, stopped teaching in Sunday School and stopped going to church.

It was during this teenage period that the first mystical experience occurred. My parents had gone out and I was alone at home one winter's evening, thinking of my doubts and arguing with myself "How can there be a God with all this evil in the world? If there is a God why does he allow people to be so wicked, and disasters like earthquakes to happen? If there isn't a God, who or what created everything anyway? And why do good people suffer when wicked people seem to get away with anything?". Such questions that have troubled humanity since the days of Job were going through my mind. I got up from my chair to poke the fire and at once, suddenly, I knew the Presence of God, ineffable, cosmic Love and yet deeply personal. Poker in hand I was transfixed. It seemed as if the earth stood still in its orbit and I could feel it breathing. An indescribable experience and the first of many such mystical experiences. It changed my life, of course, and made my faith unshakeable. Whatever happened in the future to assault my soul I would remember this and other experiences and know that all would be well.

Shortly afterwards I came in contact with the Oxford Group, which introduced me to the idea of a daily 'quiet time' as it was called. I found this very valuable, and my long-suffering parents were grateful as it meant I got up early and started the fire going before they came downstairs. I left the Oxford Group, however, shortly after it was renamed Moral Rearmament and became more politically orientated.

Early Student Days

The phrase 'It's all in the mind' has been familiar to me from a very early age. As we couldn't afford a doctor when I was a child I was told "Just go to bed and get yourself better". So I stayed in bed and talked with Jesus. But in my late teens I tried a serious experiment; on my way to art school I had a ten minute train journey, so I thought very hard 'I have a terrible splitting headache' concentrating on the thought until a real headache developed, a genuine bad one. So then I had to think the headache away again, and by the end of the journey I was free of headache and a wiser person. But my conversion to the idea of spiritual healing was very long delayed by my basic scepticism. There was an opportunity at that time to hear a famous healer speak and give a demonstration in Manchester. I no longer remember his name but I refused to go, saying it was all probably rather sinister and suspect. It took me another fifty years before I was ready to cnsider spiritual healing seriously.

Another experiment I did, based on the Gospels, was also during these early student days, just before the outbreak of war. One of the women students took a violent dislike to me and did all she could to make life unpleasant for me. I never knew why but perhaps it was because I was very critical and judgmental in my attitude. To begin with I felt resentment and wanted to retaliate, but then I remembered the admonition "Love your enemies, do good to them that persecute you" so I thought I'd try loving her. It was a difficult but valuable exercise, looking deliberately for all her good qualities (and I found plenty, to my surprise), praying for her welfare and responding only with a friendly smile to her mean actions. This went on for some months with no real conversation between us, just unspoken good will on my part. And then, out of the blue one day she came to me in the classroom and apologised for her behaviour - no explanation but we enjoyed a normal relationship after that.

Student days in Liverpool

Later in my student career the Second World War started and caused havoc in a great many lives. We had many lively debates over our easels, but the men students disappeared one by one into the forces as they were called up, all except Robert who was homosexual and a conscientious objector facing a tribunal, and then finally only the female students were left. We all had to think deeply about our attitude to the war, and while I admired the men's physical courage in going to war, facing death or injury, I also thought of their willingness to inflict death and injury on others and on balance I found more admirable Robert's moral courage in standing up for his principles against the social trend and in spite of personal abuse.

During those war-time student days in Liverpool I lived in a hostel run by the Church, as it was very near the art school and satisfied my parents' anxiety about my being away from home in a big city in wartime. The experience was illuminating. There wasn't much time or opportunity to get into any sort of trouble as the classes ran from 9am to 9pm and my only dissipation was to follow my nose (the nose was an important organ in the blackout!) to a chip shop. The other inhabitants of the hostel were interesting. One had been stranded on holiday in England and couldn't get back to her home in Australia, and a mother and daughter who were Austrians similarly stranded but because they were a German-speaking family the husband was interned in the Isle of Man. I found the daughter Hilde particularly sympathetic and she introduced me to the poetry of Rainer Maria Rilke. We enjoyed long conversations on spiritual and philosophical ideas; I also corresponded with her father in prison, and learnt that German-speaking people can be sensitive and deeply spiritual.

Sensitivity and spirituality were conspicuous by their absence in one episode that happened in that hostel. A young girl was also stranded there, working in a very menial and low-paid job in the city. One winter's day the Australian lady complained that her vest was missing from the bathroom where she had hung it to dry. So the warden decided to search our rooms and discovered that the young girl had taken the vest, her explanation being that she'd borrowed it while she washed and dried her own; she had neither money nor coupons to possess two vests. The result of this episode was that the girl was thrown out of the hostel immediately, with no compassion, no mercy shown. I'm afraid that didn't help to endear me to the Church and I left to spend the rest of my student days in a basement bed-sitter with a toilet in the back yard, and the tenants of the rest of the three-storey Victorian house would spend the nights with me during the bombing raids. That was a lesson in accepting all and sundry in a commmon need; there's no discrimination when danger threatens. And on the morning after the bombing there's no room for a student teacher's sentimentality when enquiring of the children in the class if the absentees were known to be alive or not. But my turn came to be bombed. The house was not destroyed but it was unsafe, so I had to roam the streets for the rest of the night with nothing but what I stood up in, black with soot. The greatest worry was not being able to tell my parents I was safe. There was no transport, no telephone, no power, no water, no communication of any sort. So I walked about until the college opened, dodging shrapnel and falling debris from bombed buildings, though the streets were bright and warm with all the fires. It happened in the middle of our final examinations, unfortunately, but the examiners were sympathetic and passed us all, including the student who abandoned the exam because her home was completely destroyed and her parents injured. Strangely, I can't say I felt fear at that time. It would seem that, in traumatic incidents I freeze my emotions in order to act rationally.

Teaching

As a qualified art teacher my first job was in a boarding school that was evacuated to a remote country house and estate. The education system was understandably in a state of turmoil in the early years of the war, but the school I found myself in was privately owned and quite unbelievably bad. It was so remote that communication was difficult and parents were in the forces or working away, and nobody was able to come and see what conditions their children were living in. The staff were housed in the stables with rampant rats. The local farmer grumbled that he had to pour milk down the drain because the headmistress refused to buy the children's allocation. She also censored the children's letters home. The other staff members were German or Italian, employed 'out of the goodness of her heart' she said, but at a very low salary and retained as servants during the holidays because they had got stranded in England when war broke out and consequently had neither money nor home in this country. In addition, they had the anxiety of knowing their families and homes were being bombarded though neither had any sympathy for Hitler. I should have been mature and responsible enough to report these conditions to the authorities; they amounted to child abuse and slave labour, but I'm afraid I said nothing and even profited by learning German with an authentic South German accent.

Another reason for allowing the status quo to continue without a fuss was the fact that I'd fallen in love for the first time. I was a late developer in love as in many things, so I was over twenty when it hit me for the first time. I had always previously considered boys to be juvenile and not worth my interest, but here was a young man of high ideals, gentle manners and kindly disposition. In fact, he was very like my father - how could I not love him? But I knew he didn't reciprocate my love and I had to suffer rejection, reinforcing the conviction that I was unlovable. It was difficult to keep up appearances as teaching colleagues in a boarding school but he knew my problem and was wonderfully cooperative, treating me with precisely the same courtesy as everyone else, which helped me to come to terms with the situation and avoid any occasion for gossip or awkwardness until I could move to another school.

I had lost touch with the other art students in Liverpool and never knew what happened to the men but I thought of Robert often during the next few years when I was teaching in a particularly backward part of the country. There were two churches in the village. The Anglican vicar prayed for successful bombing raids, the Methodist lay preacher seemed to think the ills of the world were due to women having been given the vote. And the headmaster, at morning assembly, would ask us to thank God for the success of our bombs in destroying Dresden and other cities. All this sickened me physically, though it had its amusing side. I learnt later that the rest of the staff would watch me going green and place bets on how long I'd hold out before dashing to the cloakroom. I believe there was even a suspicion that I might be pregnant, though it was never voiced and time proved it false anyway.

I'm not sure whether it had anything to do with my attitude to violence, but it was while teaching there that I suffered my first bout of clinical depression when everything in life was topsy-turvy. The good seemed evil and evil seemed good and there was a terrible blackness over all. Nothing I could do would shake it off. There was nobody I could confide in so I had to wear a mask of normality while suffering this black nothingness over several months. This was one of those times when I hung on to the memory of that wonderful Presence, trusting that all would be well eventually. And one winter's day I awoke to find the world outside the window covered in pure white snow, and suddenly the depression lifted. I didn't question why, but gave heartfelt thanks.

Although life returned to an even keel I was no more reconciled to the military attitudes of the school and churches, and decided to move to a more congenial atmosphere if possible. I had heard that Quakers were pacifists and, when an opportunity arose to teach in a school in St. Albans I seized it, because there was a Quaker meeting there. I felt this move was the right one for me, although I'd never met a Quaker. By this time I was seriously beginning to allow my life to be divinely guided so, to be consistent, I thought I would allow myself to be guided to the right lodgings. So, armed with a list of addresses that welcomed teachers and a street map of the town, I started to patrol the streets within walking distance of the school. At each street I would ask (whom?) "Is this the right street?" At length I came to a street where the answer was "Yes". And, of the two houses on my list for that street, again I chose to ring the bell where the answer was "Yes". The landlady and husband had a spare room because their son was away at college and the term times would fit very well with mine. It was comfortable and I settled in; on the first Sunday I took advantage of the reason for my move and went along to the Quaker meeting - and there were my landlady and her husband! I immediately felt thoroughly at home in the Quaker meeting; perhaps my earlier 'quiet times' and still earlier times spent with Jesus were good training for the Quaker hour of silent worship. In any event, the Quaker meeting for worship soon became very important to me and I never missed attending every Sunday. I felt that with the Quakers I had found my spiritual home and so I applied for formal membership as proof of my commitment. Membership is not easy - one has to apply in writing, then two members are appointed to interview the applicant and report back to the larger group, who then decide whether to accept one or not. So when someone suggested to me that I might not be accepted I replied "In that case, I shall re-apply every month until I am accepted." My lack of self esteem was producing arrogance! However, I was accepted and became an active member for the next fifty-odd years.

But although I'd found my spiritual home, life is never a bed of roses for long. There are always more lessons to be learned, so it seems I had to suffer another bout of depression. This time it was more serious, as it arose suddenly and went much deeper. I was with a friend enjoying a normal conversation at home when, happening to pass behind her for something I had a sudden and irresistable urge to put my hands around her neck and strangle her. My hands went out, almost touched her neck and then I realised with horror what I was about to do. That moment passed, inexplicable but extremely alarming. My friend never knew what had happened behind her and there was no-one I felt I could confide in, but I realised there was something within me that was capable of murder in cold blood, I had to do something about it, or there might be a next time when my hands might not withdraw in time. I could have understood perhaps if I had been furiously angry, but she was my friend and we hadn't quarelled, so the coldness in my heart really frightened me. So, by careful enquiry, I found a Jungian psychotherapist who helped, over many months of analysis, to exorcise that particular demon. Eventually I came to understand that the impulse stemmed from the moment of birth. I didn't want to be born, hated my mother for giving birth to me, suppressed the hatred and froze it into a coldness instead. Whether that was a true explanation of the event or not I felt I was cured. I was confident that I wouldn't try to strangle anyone in the future. As part of the treatment and I suspect for the doctor's benefit, he asked me to paint my feelings (I believe this was a relatively new technique at the time) and I produced a picture of extremely violent hot colours placed chaotically on the upper part of the paper, while the lower part was covered in a very thick very black and solid horizontal band. Looking at it later, it symbolised to me that 'underneath are the everlasting arms'. As I didn't feel able to confide in anyone - after all, I was teaching and I feared I might be dismissed if it was known that I was seeing a psychotherapist (mental illness was something one didn't admit to at that time). I found great help and comfort in the Book of Job and ever since then, whenever I've felt low in spirit I've turned to Job. He suffered everything possible, complained loudly but hung on to his faith and his personal relationship with God until that became a living reality in his heart as well as a rational belief.

Mature Student

As well as suppressed anger there may have been stress because of my job. I was happy enough in St Albans but not happy as a teacher. The children sensed my unease and played upon it, naturally, so I felt myself to be a failure. I also disliked an increasing bossiness in my attitude and behaviour. I'd never wanted to teach; teacher - training was part of the art course, and according to war - time regulations a trained teacher had to teach or be a conscientious objector, and at the beginning of my career when the decision had to be made I was not yet ready for that vital step.

I was attracted to the idea of taking a degree in the History of Art. It had been in my mind for a few years and I had in fact learned Latin in order to be accepted as an external student of London University. To resume study as a mature student is not easy, particularly when it is accompanied by poverty. I had saved a little from my teachers' salary and had to make it last the three years of life in London, so I rented an attic room without running water and lived as cheaply as possible, limiting my eating to six days a week and calculating which was cheaper, bus fares or shoe leather. Before the three years were over I was reduced to having cardboard in the soles of my shoes but nobody at the Quaker meeting in Hampstead suspected any of this grim determination and tenacity. I didn't see the situation in terms of problems, but only as something I had to do, no matter what. But Professor Blunt, a sensitive man, realised my difficulties and called me to his office one day to tell me that he had 'found' a special fund which would give me enough money for a month in Florence, studying the works of art. I suspected the money was coming out of his own pocket and was immensely grateful. I had never had money enough to travel abroad and my only knowledge of art works was from reproductions and descriptions. Being exposed to Florentine art for a month was a very fulfilling spiritual experience. Looking back, it links in my mind to my grandfather's admonition "If you have only enough money for a loaf of bread, buy half a loaf and a bunch of flowers", (perhaps in his time in the last century this was a feasible option!). During those three years there was neither time nor money for socialising or entertainment, and I spent my time simply studying, as I've always had a bad memory and found learning difficult. But one week I did a piece of original research which particularly pleased my tutor. Unfortunately he showed it to a well-known writer on the subject who published it as his own work without acknowledgment. I harboured some resentment about this, and realised that eminent scholars are not necessarily ethical in their actions and should only be trusted with caution. I dreaded the final examination, and worked myself up into such a state of anxiety that I left the examination hall in the middle of one paper, and went to watch the ducks in Regent's Park. Because of that and the tension I felt throughout all the papers I was not surprised when my Honours Degree was only Third Class. It was the most I deserved, but I spent the rest of the day walking the streets blindly, tears dripping down, feeling a mixture of failure and relief.

Cologne

Seeing myself as a failure as a scholar it was with some misgiving that I applied for a scholarship to Cologne University for postgraduate study. In spite of my logical self- doubts I still had the feeling of being 'led' to Cologne at this time, so I was not surprised when I was called to an interview. However, to my utter dismay, the chairman of the selection committee had a strong Berlin accent and I'd learned German from the refugee from Freiburg, so I couldn't understand him and, to add to my discomfiture, I burst into tears. Miraculously, though, I was awarded the scholarship. That year in Cologne, studying art and architecture in the Rhineland circa 1300 was an important part of my spiritual development. It introduced me to Meister Eckhart and the whole spiritual ethos of the period. The art and architecture were expressing the new 'God-within- man' spirit of the age and I felt very much in tune with it, and also with the present-day people of the Rhineland. I had dreaded what my reception might be, as an English woman whose compatriots had caused so much death and destruction only a short time before, Cologne still being a desert of rubble. But everyone was kind and welcoming, so that I felt only humility in the face of their large-heartedness. My hostess family dealt very tenderly with me when I had a spell of minor depression over a boy-friend who didn't respond to my letters. Rejection again! Although I was exposed to medieval mysticism I had no mystical experiences of my own at that time, perhaps because I was anxious about getting a job. I was in my thirties and penniless, so what would a degree in the History of Art and a year in Cologne lead to? But a letter arrived from Nikolaus Pevsner, inviting me to become his research assistant on the Penguin 'Buildings of England' series he was writing.

London Again

The work was interesting and congenial. I was responsible for collecting and organising information about the buildings of England, county by county. It meant sifting through books in reference libraries, collating the information and organising a suitable filing system. It gave me complete freedom to work in my own way and didn't tie me down to any particular place. But while I enjoyed the work I hated London, the noise, the dirt and above all the claustrophobic feel of being hemmed in by all the buildings. It taught me that at heart I was only happy with a lot of space around me, plenty of air to breathe and freedom to work as I wished.

One Sunday occurred the only mystical experience of these four years. I was in a busy restaurant, so busy that I had to share a table with three others. I had just ordered soup, and suddenly everything was transformed; the earth stood still again, as happened the first time. This lasted for several minutes, while I was completely unaware of my surroundings, and when it faded I was amazed to see that everything was as before and apparently nobody else had felt the Presence that had been in that restaurant. Otherwise my stay in London was uneventful. I was forgetting my earlier sensitivity and spiritual insights in busy-ness 'doing good' on committees and serving in office, all worthy activities but not conducive to spiritual growth or likely to lead me to that state of grace I desired. And I was also still very judgmental and tended to blame my unhappiness on London. There was also my continuing lack of self-confidence; Nikolaus Pevsner would often laugh at me indulgently at my fear of using the phone, which was ridiculous in someone in her mid-thirties. I was still very immature in many ways.

Civil Service and Marriage

But my parents were growing old and I felt I ought to be nearer to them. Also for my own sake I wanted to get out of London so, when a post was advertised for an Investigator of Historic Buildings for the North of England I applied and was accepted. So I became a Professional Civil Servant, the Ministry I worked for changing its name under successive governments though the work remained the same. It was agreed that I could use a spare room in my parents' home as my office, so all seemed to be well. But my father died almost immediately, which was a great blow as he'd given me so much of himself and his wisdom, even at the end giving me his last savings so that I could buy a car (obligatory for the job). The work was interesting and suited my temperament, as it involved travelling around looking at buildings, making reports and being free to do the work in my own way without supervision. Mother was still fit enough to be left during the day so I began to be happy again in Heysham, my old home, by the sea once more, enjoying open spaces, large skies and colourful sunsets. This however was a short interlude before the emotional turmoil of being in love. Russell, a sixty year old Quaker bachelor, met me and fell in love at first sight, he said. I was then aged 40, content with my single state and the status quo. But I came to realise that he'd awakened an emotion in me that was 'the real thing'and not to be resisted, so we had our Quaker wedding in Lancaster and a short honeymoon in Harrogate. Russell came to live with us in Heysham as I couldn't leave my mother; he was a Stockport man and a retired teacher, so he was free to move. I continued with my work and Russell accompanied me on my travels, so we were constantly together. Marrying so late in life made us both aware that we couldn't hope for very many years together, so every moment was precious. He was a rare husband. To him I was always beautiful, talented and wise, and his faith in me was so strong that I was inspired to believe more in myself and act with more self- assurance. His loving spirit and his heart-warming joyous laugh remain in my memory. But the greatest lesson he taught me was in the manner of his dying. Never having suffered a day's illness in his life before, he had a massive heart attack and knew he was dying. He lingered for five weeks, his strength gradually waning. When the doctor told me that death was near, Doris, my friend for 35 years, came to share the night watches. At his conscious intervals he was, as always, loving, contented and full of fun (he remarked once on all his 'concubines' when he saw the woman doctor, the District Nurse, Doris and me all around his bed). I was with him in the final hours, and in his last conscious moments he smiled at me with such heart-breaking sweetness and said, haltingly and feebly, but triumphantly "Our love is indestructible. It is part of the eternal love of God. We shan't be parted. Only for a little while in the reckoning of Eternity." Some time later he appeared to be conscious again. His eyes were wide open and intelligent; I spoke to him but he was not aware of my presence. Instead, he kept looking round the room as if he were following some moving object or large crowd in front of him. His eyes kept returning to a point in the centre, and the expression in them can only be described as pure wonder, I was very aware in that moment of a divine Presence, come to take Russell's spirit. It was almost unendurable, and I cried out that I should be taken too - Russell and I had always shared everything - but I was gently and firmly shut out from this experience. I grieved of course. Russell had given me the 10 happiest years of my life; he'd given me self-respect and self-confidence, and made me feel that at last I was lovable. But life had to go on.

Mother had already died some years before, also of a heart attack but suddenly and fatally while I was absent, and so now I was quite alone with no family and no relatives. Work was a great help, but the evenings spent alone in hotels when working away in the North-East of England were very trying. It had been fun when Russell was with me but the enjoyment had gone out of the work. It was the early 1970's when a lone woman in a hotel was a rarity and I suffered the humiliation of being ignored by waiters until, with my new-found confidence, I learnt to demand attention. I received more attention than I wanted from the'reps' who normally frequented the hotels. There were two kinds I discovered after several after-dinner experiences. There were those who treated me as an agony aunt and told me how misunderstood they were by their wives or undervalued by their boss. And there were those who pinned me down and forced me to admire all the photos, achievements and exploits of every member of their family. So I was at last driven to staying all evening in my bedroom - not conducive to recovery from grief. At least I had learnt more about human nature though compassion for others was not on my agenda at that time. I needed distraction. I tried the local corner shop thinking they might have a book of crosswords but 'by chance' I picked up a paperback 'Teach Yourself Esperanto'. I thought at the time that it would either send me to sleep through boredom or it would distract my mind away from my loss. But of course it was no accident that I found that particular book. I was still being 'led' though I was not in a state to be conscious of it, nor was I aware of the far - reaching consequences. Far from sending me to sleep I found Esperanto an absorbing language which immediately opened up a whole world of new friendships and contacts. I started corresponding with people in many countries, gaining insight into other customs, other lifestyles, other points of view. My horizons widened and I realised there was more to life than work, however congenial, and earning a living, so I retired early from my job and had the luxury of time to myself instead of the luxury of a monthly salary.

International Work

Again a new beginning and a fresh adventure. As with so many experiences, there was pain as well as pleasure involved. The pleasure came in the many contacts I made and the enjoyable journeys in various countries of Europe, talking to Esperanto groups about Quakerism and talking to Quaker groups about Esperanto. By that time I was a fluent speaker in Esperanto and began also to teach it. In spite of my efforts I was unable to persuade any Quakers to learn the language, though I found Esperantists more open to receive new ideas. Travelling about, meeting new people and speaking at public meetings were all new to me and helped to develop my new-found and Russell-inspired self-confidence. But the most thrilling experiences were the international conferences, held each year in a different country (e g in 1999 Germany) and attended by thousands of people from over 50 countries, all able to talk to one another on equal terms linguistically. These were truly inspiring events. But the most memorable one I attended was in Iceland, when an excursion took some of us by bus to the still-hot ashes of the Mount Hekla eruption, where I stood with awe on the steaming origins of the earth, as it seemed. I was aware of the immense power beneath my feet, of the molten fiery energy at the centre of the earth. And only a few miles away was the huge Vatna Jokull glacier whose cold melt waters met the warmer ocean water and gave a home to two totally different kinds of fish. I had always been aware of the beauty of nature and loved to paint landscapes, but this was something different, like being present at the beginning of Creation - totally awe-inspiring . Since then I've had several experiences, notably in the Scottish Highlands, when my feet seem to descend and become one with the centre of the earth - a warming experience as I normally have cold feet!

More heart-warming was the experience of co-operating with nine others in translating an English novel into Esperanto so that it would have a world wide readership. We were all members of the Morecambe Bay Esperanto Group and worked at home on two chapters each, coming together weekly to harmonise our style. Our translation was printed and published to coincide with the British Esperanto

Conference being held in Morecambe, at which event I had to preside as the local representative. I know I couldn't have done any of this without Russell's faith in me; although the ability may have been there it was certainly dormant until awakened by his love and strengthened by my daily habit of meditation.

Although I had travelled in various European countries I feel I was particularly led to Poland, though in a devious way. It happened that a Buddhist monk in Tokyo suggested to his Polish pen-friend that he (the Pole) should write to me about his philosophical and religious ideas. So I gained another Esperantist friend and we corresponded for some time. And then the Polish government (Communist) offered a grant to a British woman who would like to study how they were restoring their historic buildings after the war. The subject certainly interested me and thankfully I was awarded the grant. But instead of contacting government officials I contacted Esperantists in the towns I wished to visit, principally Warsaw and Krakow. So I had the privilege of living for a while in Polish homes and learning what life was like for ordinary Poles during and after the war. And, at the end of my visit I had a couple of days to spare so I went to see my pen-friend Adam and his family in Silesia. Unfortunately Adam died suddenly shortly afterwards but my visit was the start of a very rewarding and long lasting friendship with his widow Halina and son Darek. I am particularly indebted to Darek, a young man with Down's syndrome, as he's taught me so much about acceptance and thankfulness. He is a person who seems to have a relationship with God which is totally natural and truly childlike. I for one always feel special in his presence, and a better person for having met him.

At home in Heysham other events were to have less happy consequences, however. For some time British Esperantists had wanted to open an international guest-house, and property had been found in Heysham. This was owned and run by a committee drawn from around the country, from Scotland to the south of England. This was perhaps our main mistake as I, being the only local committee member, was left to do the work of running the 8-bedroomed hotel. We were all volunteers of course, but for me it meant working 24 hours a day seven days a week. I attended a course in hotel management in order to offer an efficient service, and employed a cook for evening meals. I was very happy meeting all the people who came to stay, but it was exhausting work and I began to resent the fact that the other members of the committee left all decisions and all the work to me. This situation continued for some years until it was noticeable that a crack in one wall was widening. The upshot was, after exhaustive and expensive tests, the hotel was found to be built on shifting sand and was unsafe. So all our work and hopes were in vain. The property was sold at a loss and again I was angry and resentful that nobody came to help to wind up the business; at the end I had to threaten to put all the files, books etc. on the street if nobody came to collect them before my removal from Heysham. In the event someone came at the very last minute, but I was too exhausted by then even to be angry any more. Perhaps it was because of my anger that I became ill at the end and had to take to my bed (a rare event for me). But that's another part of the story. I have realised since that it was unreasonable to expect any close co-operation from such a widely scattered group, and we were all equally at fault for setting up such an unworkable committee in the first place. And I had let my enthusiasm run away with me, beyond reason. So that was an unhappy end to my 60 years association with Heysham.

The Isle of Arran

But the lesson had been learnt and unhappiness doesn't last forever. During those last months I had occasion to visit the Isle of Arran, on behalf of a friend who wished to have a preliminary opinion of a property for sale before he took time off work to go and seriously consider buying it. I offered to go because of my abiding interest in houses and I'd never been to Arran, so the visit would satisfy my wanderlust at the same time. I was ever ready for a fresh adventure but was not prepared for the strange feeling I had on the ferry crossing from Ardrossan. It was a very strong feeling, a conviction even, that I was 'coming home'. The feeling remained with me during the very wet 24 hours I spent on Arran, to such an extent that on my return to Heysham I started the process of selling my home there. In the event my friend didn't manage to buy a property on Arran, but I did!

As mentioned previously, I became ill before leaving Heysham and was still in bed with the doctor attending the day before the removal. My Polish friend Halina (an invaluable help in packing and unpacking) was concerned that I wasn't fit to drive the two hundred miles to the ferry but, remembering that 'it's all in the mind' the journey was accomplished, my spirits rising with every mile. Arran was the perfect place to relax, unwind, and absorb the peace and beauty that are its dominant characteristics. For three years I did just that, becoming inspired by the beauty to start painting again. However, although I was happy living an idle life, painting and enjoying the many new friendships, I felt there was something lacking. I was being selfish and felt guilty that I was giving nothing back to society. Feeling somewhat low in spirit I enrolled for a weekend's healing course in Surrey, thinking I would receive some healing for my soul, but instead I found that I myself had a gift for hands-on healing. It wasn't what I expected to happen but I felt obliged then to develop the gift through a course of training, and use it to help anyone who needed me. So the healing work began, both the healing of myself and the healing I could convey to others. I was then in my seventies but the new career was to develop further, with training in Hypnotherapy, Regression and Past life (or Reincarnation) Therapy. All these seemed to follow naturally from the healing, as I felt it was necessary to help the client find the cause of his/her problem, face it emotionally and so complete the healing process. In effect, I see the aim of my work as helping the client to find his/her own soul and help it on its journey to the Source. As part of my training I had been regressed many times - hence the six lives in Part One - but there were other occasions when I regressed not to a past life but to a past post-death experience. These occasions were wonderful mystical experiences, a development of my previous conscious experiences. It is clear to me that death in most cases is less stressful than birth. My own case is not exceptional; we don't want to be born because we are leaving the wonderful Light and Love of the between-lives state, so soon to be forgotten in the trauma of living and learning, whereas death is a return to that state of Light and Love. In some instances I have experienced a Darkness beyond the Light, beyond yet within the Light, and beyond that again I've found myself helping to create stars, beautiful pin-points of dancing light, like a divine ballet, in ever-changing patterns of scintillating colour. These mystical experiences make me yearn to return to that state. There is certainly no cause for fear. Perhaps I became obsessional, but in 1997 I had a strong feeling that I was to die later that year. This I welcomed and prepared for, clearing away all the accumulated 'junk' in my life. I spent the day of my expected death in meditation, with occasional visions and the awareness of 'presences', but I remained alive at the end of the day! In spite of this disappointment I still felt there was something 'right' about the episode, which proved to be the case. After about three months of mourning for a self that had died that day, I received a tremendous new influx of energy, truly a resurrection to a new freer self. And part of that energy has been utilised in the writing of this book, though as soon as the energy is used it is renewed, in a constant flow from the Cosmic Source.

My most recent regression experience revealed an agony comparable to that of my first recorded life (Chapter 1). Then, it was the unbearable agony of not being able to accept Love in its fullness. This time it was the unbearable agony of the world's suffering. I thought I couldn't bear it and cried out with the pain, but this time I didn't commit suicide. Instead,

I came to realise that both are but facets of the same. Love must include suffering, to deny one is to deny the other. As in my vision of the after-death state, Light includes Darkness, and beyond both is Creation.

The journey to the Source of Love continues.

Epilogue

I had thought to write a final chapter, tying together all the strands of the previous chapters and, like a Victorian novel, pointing out the moral at the end of the story. But the story has no end and there is no 'moral' which ties it all together. Instead I invite you, the intelligent and sensitive reader, to turn back to any portion of the story that seems to have a message especially for you, and ponder its significance for your spiritual life. It is your story as well as mine, and you have your own lessons to learn. If you can learn from my mistakes, so be it. My wish is that my experiences may give you hope and freedom from the fear of death.